T0287445

Penguin Monarchs

THE HOUSES OF WESSEX AND DENMARK

Athelstan*	Tom Holland
Aethelred the Unready	Richard Abels
Cnut	Ryan Lavelle
Edward the Confessor	David Woodman

THE HOUSES OF NORMANDY, BLOIS AND ANJOU

William I*	Marc Morris
William II	John Gillingham
Henry I	Edmund King
Stephen	Carl Watkins
Henry II*	Richard Barber
Richard I	Thomas Asbridge
John	Nicholas Vincent

THE HOUSE OF PLANTAGENET

Henry III	Stephen Church
Edward I*	Andy King
Edward II	Christopher Given-Wilson
Edward III*	Jonathan Sumption
Richard II*	Laura Ashe

THE HOUSES OF LANCASTER AND YORK

Henry IV	Catherine Nall
Henry V*	Anne Curry
Henry VI	James Ross
Edward IV	A. J. Pollard
Edward V	Thomas Penn
Richard III	Rosemary Horrox

* Now in paperback

THE HOUSE OF TUDOR

Henry VII	Sean Cunningham
Henry VIII*	John Guy
Edward VI*	Stephen Alford
Mary I*	John Edwards
Elizabeth I	Helen Castor

THE HOUSE OF STUART

James I	Thomas Cogswell
Charles I*	Mark Kishlansky
[Cromwell*	David Horspool]
Charles II*	Clare Jackson
James II	David Womersley
William III & Mary II*	Jonathan Keates
Anne	Richard Hewlings

THE HOUSE OF HANOVER

George I	Tim Blanning
George II	Norman Davies
George III	Amanda Foreman
George IV	Stella Tillyard
William IV	Roger Knight
Victoria*	Jane Ridley

THE HOUSES OF SAXE-COBURG & GOTHA AND WINDSOR

Edward VII*	Richard Davenport-Hines
George V*	David Cannadine
Edward VIII*	Piers Brendon
George VI*	Philip Ziegler
Elizabeth II*	Douglas Hurd

* Now in paperback

STELLA TILLYARD

George IV

King in Waiting

ALLEN LANE
an imprint of
PENGUIN BOOKS

ALLEN LANE

UK | USA | Canada | Ireland | Australia
India | New Zealand | South Africa

Penguin Books is part of the Penguin Random House group of companies
whose addresses can be found at global.penguinrandomhouse.com

First published 2019
001

Copyright © Stella Tillyard, 2019

The moral right of the author has been asserted

Set in 9.5/13.5 pt Sabon LT Std
Typeset by Jouve (UK), Milton Keynes
Printed and bound in Great Britain by Clays Ltd, Elcograf S.p.A.

ISBN: 978-0-141-97885-7

Contents

HOUSE OF HANOVER

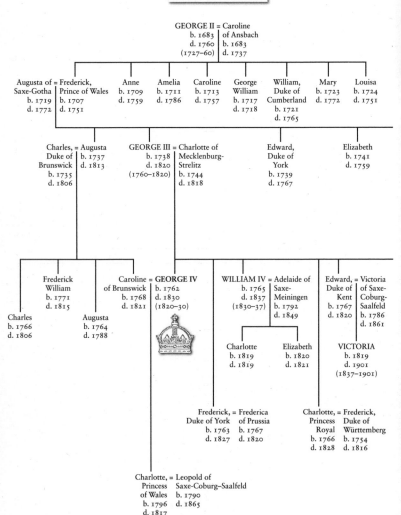

GEORGE II = Caroline
b. 1683 | of Ansbach
d. 1760 | b. 1683
(1727–60) | d. 1737

Augusta of = Frederick,
Saxe-Gotha | Prince of Wales
b. 1719 | b. 1707
d. 1772 | d. 1751

Anne
b. 1709
d. 1759

Amelia
b. 1711
d. 1786

Caroline
b. 1713
d. 1757

George
William
b. 1717
d. 1718

William,
Duke of
Cumberland
b. 1721
d. 1765

Mary
b. 1723
d. 1772

Louisa
b. 1724
d. 1751

Charles, = Augusta
Duke of | b. 1737
Brunswick | d. 1813
b. 1735
d. 1806

GEORGE III = Charlotte of
b. 1738 | Mecklenburg-
d. 1820 | Strelitz
(1760–1820) | b. 1744
| d. 1818

Edward,
Duke of
York
b. 1739
d. 1767

Elizabeth
b. 1741
d. 1759

Charles
b. 1766
d. 1806

Frederick
William
b. 1771
d. 1815

Augusta
b. 1764
d. 1788

Caroline
of Brunswick
b. 1768
d. 1821

GEORGE IV
b. 1762
d. 1830
(1820–30)

WILLIAM IV = Adelaide of
b. 1765 | Saxe-
d. 1837 | Meiningen
(1830–37) | b. 1792
| d. 1849

Edward, = Victoria
Duke of | of Saxe-
Kent | Coburg-
b. 1767 | Saalfeld
d. 1820 | b. 1786
| d. 1861

Charlotte
b. 1819
d. 1819

Elizabeth
b. 1820
d. 1821

VICTORIA
b. 1819
d. 1901
(1837–1901)

Frederick, = Frederica
Duke of York | of Prussia
b. 1763 | b. 1767
d. 1827 | d. 1820

Charlotte, = Frederick,
Princess | Duke of
Royal | Württemberg
b. 1766 | b. 1754
d. 1828 | d. 1816

Charlotte, = Leopold of
Princess | Saxe-Coburg–Saalfeld
of Wales | b. 1790
b. 1796 | d. 1865
d. 1817

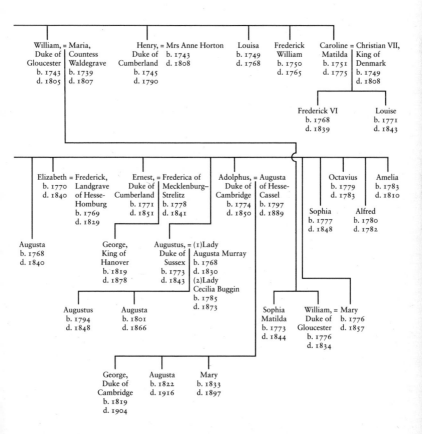

William, = Maria,
Duke of | Countess
Gloucester | Waldegrave
b. 1743 | b. 1739
d. 1805 | d. 1807

Henry, = Mrs Anne Horton
Duke of | b. 1743
Cumberland | d. 1808
b. 1745
d. 1790

Louisa
b. 1749
d. 1768

Frederick
William
b. 1750
d. 1765

Caroline = Christian VII,
Matilda | King of
b. 1751 | Denmark
d. 1775 | b. 1749
| d. 1808

Frederick VI
b. 1768
d. 1839

Louise
b. 1771
d. 1843

Elizabeth = Frederick,
b. 1770 | Landgrave
d. 1840 | of Hesse-
| Homburg
| b. 1769
| d. 1829

Ernest, = Frederica of
Duke of | Mecklenburg–
Cumberland | Strelitz
b. 1771 | b. 1778
d. 1851 | d. 1841

Adolphus, = Augusta
Duke of | of Hesse-
Cambridge | Cassel
b. 1774 | b. 1797
d. 1850 | d. 1889

Octavius
b. 1779
d. 1783

Amelia
b. 1783
d. 1810

Sophia
b. 1777
d. 1848

Alfred
b. 1780
d. 1782

Augusta
b. 1768
d. 1840

George,
King of
Hanover
b. 1819
d. 1878

Augustus, = (1)Lady
Duke of | Augusta Murray
Sussex | b. 1768
b. 1773 | d. 1830
d. 1843 | (2)Lady
| Cecilia Buggin
| b. 1785
| d. 1873

Augustus
b. 1794
d. 1848

Augusta
b. 1801
d. 1866

Sophia
Matilda
b. 1773
d. 1844

William, = Mary
Duke of | b. 1776
Gloucester | d. 1857
b. 1776
d. 1834

George,
Duke of
Cambridge
b. 1819
d. 1904

Augusta
b. 1822
d. 1916

Mary
b. 1833
d. 1897

George IV

I

Father and Son

When he was told by a harassed courtier that his wife had successfully delivered their first child, a girl, on the evening of 12 August 1762, the young King George III was overcome with relief. He was 'but little anxious as to the sex of the Child', he said. The important thing was that Queen Charlotte was safe. Running into the queen's bedchamber in St James's Palace, he was greeted with a surprise. He found that his daughter was in fact a son and heir, a 'strong, large, pretty Boy'.[1] The king and his eighteen-year-old wife were delighted. Relations between the monarch and his son were never as equable or as good again.

Sixty-seven years later, on 26 June 1830, King George IV, that same large and pretty boy, died at Windsor Castle, a sick recluse unmourned by the nation. The *Times* leader, published a day after his funeral, declared that 'there never was an individual less regretted by his fellow-creatures than this deceased King'. 'What eye has wept for him?' it asked rhetorically. 'What heart has heaved one throb of unmercenary sorrow? . . . If George IV ever had a friend – a devoted friend – in any rank of life,' the paper concluded, 'we protest that the name of him or her has not yet reached us.'[2]

As Prince of Wales and then as Regent, George's place in

the world was defined first by his being heir to the throne, but second, and more importantly, by the personality and presence of his father. There had been plenty of scapegrace princes before George, plenty of young men who defied their fathers and rebelled against the rules they laid down. The future George II had hated, and been hated by, his father, George I, and then reproduced that hostile relationship with his own son Frederick, Prince of Wales, the father of George III. Frederick died in 1751 when his own heir was only twelve years old, too young to have any sort of independent life. Yet despite having avoided the Hanoverian pattern of a combative relationship with his own father, George III was particularly strict and unforgiving himself. While he was able to do so, he laid down stringent rules about what his heir could and could not do, and effectively condemned his son to a regal half-life. First and foremost, Prince George was to be the Prince of Wales, the next king; but in the meantime, while neither a private gentleman nor a monarch, he was circumscribed by his father's diktats, unable to decide where to go, whom to marry or, in theory, what to spend.

The prince's life was also defined by the ubiquity and boldness of the mid-eighteenth-century press, which never hesitated to print every scrap of news and gossip about him that it could find. Though the law of libel was increasingly used to gag criticism, it was still weak enough for satirists and cartoonists to wreak merry havoc with the royal family in a way that would be unthinkable in today's more deferential age. In 1812, at the beginning of the Regency, the essayist Charles Lamb could lampoon the portly Regent as the 'Prince of Whales' in a long poem in the *Examiner* that was half joke, half satire. Some of the kinder lines ran:

> Not a mightier whale than this
> In the vast Atlantic is;
> Not a fatter fish than he
> Flounders round the polar sea.[3]

Real privacy for a member of the royal family was impossible in an era of such press freedom. With no occupation, as Prince of Wales, George was forced to live as a semi-private gentleman, yet without the protections that a respectful or cowed press might afford. Moreover, as if a rampant press wasn't enough, George's maturity coincided with the beginnings of a golden age of memoir and biography. He was surrounded day and night by people who knew the value, in both fame and money, of their observations and recollections. Courtiers, servants and all kinds of visitors: no one hesitated to make the most of their gleanings. As a consequence, we probably know more about the prince's private habits, at least as they were observed by others, than those of any other monarch.

George's great quest as Prince of Wales was to find something to do that could give him a purpose while he waited for his father to die. The story of his life from birth until the advent of the Regency in 1811 was his failure to find anything that matched his talents, engrossed his attention and could be pursued with the dignity that his situation demanded. Watched by anxious nurses, tutors and parents and never unattended as a child, George was unable to learn how to be at peace with himself. Much of his behaviour was conditioned by his horror of solitude, his inability to tolerate the boredom that came with his role and his impatience with the constraints this situation laid upon him.

It all started as well as possible. Though George III preferred girls to boys, he was a fond father to all his babies. A great line of children followed the Prince of Wales into the world – eight boys and six girls – so that no worry about providing an heir ever hung over the royal household. The king dearly wished for a warm domestic life of the sort that he himself had lacked after the death of his father, when he had been removed from his mother to endure an adolescence of awkward seclusion. As soon as he inherited the throne ten years later in 1760, George set about finding a suitable woman to marry. Though constrained by having to look outside Britain into Protestant Europe, so that his bride would arrive unencumbered by any family ambitions, he and his mother quickly settled on seventeen-year-old Charlotte, a younger daughter of the Duke of Mecklenburg-Strelitz. Strelitz was a tiny agricultural duchy in northern Germany, where Charlotte was growing up in rural isolation, in the midst of a loving family and far away from the intrigues of a large court. The Duke of Mecklenburg-Strelitz, according to a visitor in the mid 1730s, liked nothing better than a bit of sewing, and had perfected the art of embroidering his own dressing gowns, while his wife and daughters cheerfully darned stockings at the dinner table.[4] Despite this modest eccentricity, Princess Charlotte received a conventional, thoroughly Protestant education, from which she emerged with a smattering of French and Latin, a good deal of theology and a lifelong love of music and botany. She grew up bookish but not questioning, once returning a volume of Voltaire to its owner with the comment: 'I do not want anything more of his.'[5]

This conventionality, together with the untainted provincialism of Charlotte's upbringing, was just what George III was looking for in a wife and companion. It did not matter that Charlotte was regarded as thin and extremely plain. Far more important were her lack of pretension and her acceptance of his authority. George wanted a wife who would not meddle, as he put it, and, from the moment she arrived in London, Charlotte never did. She had much to endure, but rarely dared to show any regret for the life she had lost, except in letters to her elder brother Charles, safely distant in Strelitz, and to whom she wrote despairingly at a low point in 1778: 'ah, my dear brother, how many thorns a great rank has! There are many bitter pills to swallow; the very fact of being surrounded by people to whom one cannot become attached, even if one wanted to, is enough to repel a soul as sensitive as mine.'[6]

Despite his German wife and a court at which German and French were frequently spoken, George III was determined to make the monarchy British and provincial. At a time when British aristocrats, especially in the households of the dominant Whigs, were revelling in sentiment and extravagance of all sorts, followed French taste and fashion and travelled extensively on the continent, where they bought every luxury in sight, the king was moving the other way. He prized restraint and demanded moderation in all things, especially in the consumption and display of strong feeling. Family life and rituals – and later the pastimes of the countryside – set the tone and hours in his household. As the children increased in numbers, it soon resembled that of his widowed mother much more closely than that of his card-playing grandfather George II, who had lived with his mistress Lady Yarmouth in Kensington Palace amid all the old-fashioned ritual of a continental court.

George III wanted a family household sequestered from the corrupting influence of the city and the court, and selected Buckingham House at the end of Pall Mall in which to make it. Then, as his family grew, he moved it each summer to various houses in and around the Green at Kew, where he himself had lived until his father died. With these decisions, as with all others, the queen was expected to comply; and she did, never openly defying her husband in almost sixty years of marriage. There was a stultifying atmosphere in all these households, and courtiers were often driven to distraction with boredom. Despite the king's best intentions, the warmth that he had so much wanted proved elusive. Queen Charlotte was an exemplary mother and wife, but never a relaxed or happy person. In 1780, after eighteen years of pregnancy and childbirth, she confided to her brother that 'I have need of all my religion to support myself in this situation', but the effort of self-control 'has a strange effect on me, and prevents me from enjoying even the small amount of pleasure I have. For God knows, there is a small amount at present, and it gets less day by day.'[7]

During the first nine years of his life, Prince George was burdened more with the weight of his many names and titles than with a strict education. He quickly grew into a good-looking child, with a mass of light brown hair and fine grey-blue eyes. He was looked after by a crew of wet-nurses and female courtiers and servants and given plenty of physical affection, especially by his father, who loved to get down on the carpet and play with his children when they were young. Early on, the young prince was notable for his good memory, imagination and intelligence. At the age of three and a half, when he was asked if he was bored by having to stay in bed after his smallpox inoculation, he replied, 'Not at all, I lye and make Reflections.'[8] By the time he was five he had started lessons in reading, writing and grammar. At six he wrote his first letter.

Reading and writing were balanced by the kinds of activities advocated by the Swiss philosopher Jean-Jacques Rousseau in his best-selling educational tract *Émile, ou De l'éducation*, published in 1762. These included plenty of contact with nature and learning through fashionable games, such as Madame de Beaumont's jigsaw puzzle maps, which could be assembled into countries and continents. The royal teachers, in particular Lady Charlotte Finch, were devoted to their charges. George was petted, loved and praised. Surrounded by an ever-growing tribe of brothers and sisters, he maintained an easy superiority by virtue not just of his talents but also of his rank, which predisposed those around him in his favour.

The early 1770s were very difficult years for the king and the monarchy of which he was the head. His restless American subjects were testing the bonds that tied them to the mother country. In December 1773, their grievances exploded in the spectacle of the Boston Tea Party, when a group of Bostonians dressed as Mohawk Indians boarded tea ships in the port of Boston and tipped their cargos into the harbour in protest at the imposition of import duty. George III regarded himself as the father of all his subjects, and so he saw American assertiveness as both a familial and a political failure.

This colonial insubordination was accompanied by a series of blows from the king's own wayward siblings. First came the shame and ridicule that followed the court action for criminal conversation taken out by Earl Grosvenor against Prince Henry in spring 1770, after the prince had been discovered in flagrante with the earl's wife in a bedroom of the White Hart Inn at St Albans. In 1771, Prince Henry compounded this embarrassment, during which the public were delighted by the printing of his ludicrous and badly spelled love letters, with a hasty and secret marriage to a commoner. This enraged the king, who saw it as his duty to direct both the public and private lives of all his siblings as well as his children. Anticipating by several years Prince Henry's misconduct, the king's favourite brother, Prince William, Duke of Gloucester, had concealed his own secret marriage, but had to make it public the following year, in 1772, when his wife became pregnant. Worst of all, the king's youngest sister, Caroline Matilda, Queen of Denmark, was arrested in the Royal Palace at Copenhagen in January 1772, accused of adultery with a German doctor. She was imprisoned in Kronborg Castle in Helsingør – the grim fortress of Elsinore in Shakespeare's *Hamlet* – and it took months of diplomatic wrangling and threats of war to get her out.

The king was mortified and disgusted by his siblings'

behaviour. Their refusal to recognize his familial authority would give licence to other members of the family and all his subjects to defy him in the same way. In the heat of the affair of Prince Henry, the king declared that he could offer no leniency and must show his resentment. He himself had children, he explained, 'who must know what they have to expect if they could follow so infamous an example'.[9]

The immediate public result of his brothers' secret marriages was the Royal Marriages Act, passed later in 1772, which gave the king control of the marriage choices of his brothers and sisters and children until they were twenty-five years old. The effect was to make the king more than ever fearful in private of the baleful influence of the world on his children, even though the Prince of Wales was then only nine years old.

George III decided that his eldest son needed a more rigorous and disciplined way of living if he was to be able to arm himself against the worldly temptations that had brought such disgrace to the family and the nation. So, in 1773, the congenial family life that the prince had enjoyed came abruptly to an end. George and his younger brother Frederick were removed from the rest of the royal family and set up in Kew Palace under the eye of a governor, Lord Holdernesse, and several tutors. Hugs and kisses were withdrawn. For the next seven years, the two princes were subjected to a routine of unvaried scholarly discipline, enforced by beatings if they were lazy or untruthful. Their governors and tutors changed over the years, but not the timetable of their days, which consisted of hours of instruction in religion, morals, government and law, interspersed with modern and ancient languages and a few more recent texts. The only British writers the princes studied were Shakespeare, Milton and Pope. For exercise the princes rode out together or with the king, and they were encouraged to dig the earth and grow vegetables and crops, as Rousseau prescribed.

Although the prince later impressed visitors with his literary knowledge, and was good at recycling the learning of his youth, his fear of being alone prevented him from being a serious reader, at least until his later years, when infirmity often confined him indoors and he took to reading in bed. In his youth, he was much better suited to music, by talent and temperament, becoming a good cello player and proficient at the piano. Playing and listening to music offered and brought conviviality and, later, when he had developed a taste for popular songs, fun. He was a good mimic and picked up a melody with ease.

The princes were permitted few other pastimes in their seclusion at Kew. Frequent letters from the king urging study, religious devotion and duty to him as their father and king can only have dampened their spirits, especially when, during difficult political times, George III seemed to demand that his own burdens be lightened by his sons' demonstrating good behaviour. 'I cannot conclude,' the king wrote in 1778, soon after the French had officially entered the American Revolutionary War, 'without just adding that I know very well I have a difficult time to steer the helm, but the confidence I place in Divine Providence, the attachment I have for this my native country, and the love I bear my children, are insentatives [incentives] sufficient to make me strain every nerf to do my duty ... Act uprightly and shew the anxious care I have had of you has not been misspent.'[10]

From the very beginning, George chafed against the king's demands and restrictions. He resented the emotional weight his father placed on him, the endless hours of schoolwork, the infantilizing clothes he was forced to wear, and the lack of diversion. None the less, whenever he met outsiders, especially in Frederick's company, they were invariably charmed by him and compared him favourably to his younger brother. The Prince of Wales, wrote one visitor, was 'not so handsome as his brother, but his countenance was of a sweetness and intelligence quite irresistible. He had an elegant person, engaging and distinguished manners, added to an affectionate disposition and the cheerfulness of youth. In accomplishments the brothers were unequal, as well as in acquired knowledge, the scale turning always in favour of the Prince of Wales.'[11]

The prince himself enthusiastically seconded this good opinion. At seventeen, he dashed off a paean of self-praise to one of his sisters' attendants, describing himself in the third person. 'His sentiments & thoughts are open and generous,' he wrote, 'above doing anything that is mean ... grateful and friendly to excess where he finds *a real friend*. His heart is good & tender if it is allowed to show its emotions.' He admitted to vices 'or rather let us call them weaknesses', and to being 'rather too fond of Wine and Women'. He acknowledged that he was 'too subject to be in a passion'; but since 'he never bears malice or rancour in his heart', his quick temper was forgivable.[12]

Partly as a result of this surround sound of approbation, which stood in such contrast to his own memories of a lonely adolescence and a costive and cold mother, George III gradually became envious of his gregarious, easy, unzipped and emotionally entitled son. It was impossible for the king to admit to such a feeling, however: the idea of himself as an honest, straightforward and honourable man was central to his self-image. So his envy came out as disapproval and disdain, sentiments that the prince, equally wedded to his idea of himself as generous and kind, returned. It was an unresolvable relationship on both sides, and both men were the poorer for it. George III took refuge in self-righteous hurt, the prince in high living and indulgence.

It wasn't long before commentators and cartoonists cheerfully echoed this definition by contrasts, making it all the more difficult for either to change himself or his relationship with the other. Cartoonists routinely portrayed the king as skinny and mean, a simply dressed countryman, Farmer George, who ate soup or a single boiled egg for supper, sitting opposite his scrawny queen. The Prince of Wales was shown as an unbuttoned voluptuary dedicated to wine, women, loose company, extravagance and any available forms of fashionable excess.

In 1780, when the prince was eighteen, the king gave permission for him to set up his own establishment, as was customary, though while the prince now had his own staff, he did not yet have his own household. New apartments were prepared for him, but they were right under the king's eye, both at Buckingham House and at Windsor. As soon as the Prince of Wales had moved into this new establishment, his younger brother Prince Frederick was unceremoniously despatched to Hanover to complete his military education.

His removal left George bereft of his only childhood companion and dangerously alone. From this point on, the prince fixed himself even more resolutely against his father, and so the baleful Hanoverian pattern of enmity between monarch and heir was set in motion again. George III took every opportunity to denigrate his son, writing with a self-serving combination of blame and hurt just two days after his son's eighteenth birthday: 'Your own good sense must make you feel that you have not made that progress in your studies which, from the ability and assiduity of those placed for that purpose about you, I might have had reason to expect.' The king 'hates me', the prince later told his friend James Harris, adding: 'he always did, from seven years old'.[13]

In the early 1780s, as he approached his majority, the prince's character and form began to assume their mature contours. He was charming, but unreliable; often in high spirits, but as often histrionic, particularly when he did not get his own way. He could be gracious, was naturally socially adroit and skilled at putting visitors at their ease. His instincts were always on the side of gentleness. He was kindly to children and to his sisters, who were growing up miserably sequestered at Kew and, later, Windsor; he was unafraid of sentimentality and hated cruelty towards animals. When he was king, he shrank at any discussion of the execution of criminals, which he had to approve, and always preferred leniency. 'It not unfrequently happens that a culprit escapes owing to the scruples of the King,' an observer noted.[14]

Yet all these winning qualities were offset by a reluctance to perform any tasks that were uncongenial. Conditioned by entitlement on one side and by a lack of true affection on the other, his life was uneasy and performative. He was very ready to forget the rank of people he met, a habit described by contemporaries as 'condescension' or 'easy manners', but they were required always to remember his. In the same way, he was fond of practical jokes and loved to mimic others, but never forgave anyone who teased him in return, especially about his weight, which began to increase rapidly in his twenties.

The public role of the Prince of Wales was ill-defined. George III had inherited the throne from his grandfather when he was twenty-two and had never had to live as an adult in the shadow of his father. Yet this time round, the Prince of Wales could reasonably expect to inhabit his role for decades. When George was eighteen, his father the king was only forty-two. The question then was, what to do?

The role of Prince of Wales demanded above all patience, discretion and duty, to none of which George was naturally inclined. An old friend, Lady Holland, summed up the dilemma in which his character was caught. There was 'more good in him than falls to the lot of most Princes', she wrote, and 'had he not been one, he would, I am persuaded, have been a most amiable man'.[15]

In August 1783, the Prince of Wales attained his majority. Although he had no official duties, he was now in a very public way his father's heir and George III expected him to act with the decorum and ceremony his position demanded. Unfortunately for the king, the prince now also acquired a household and full establishment of his own, along with a Civil List income that, after much protest from the king, was fixed at £50,000 a year. To this burden on the taxpayers was added £12,000 a year from the Duchy of Cornwall, which by tradition came to the Prince of Wales, and a supposedly one-off capital sum of £60,000 that was provided directly by Parliament. For a residence, the prince was given use of Carlton House on the southern side of Pall Mall, which had been occupied by the king's mother, Augusta, until her death a decade earlier. It was an undistinguished house, but sat in a very large, fine garden. Suitably for the prince's habits, it awaited a complete renovation and revamp.

Everything was now set up for the multiple forms of rebellion that the prince was to play out. With his Civil List and Duchy of Cornwall income, his own household and a large and potentially sumptuous house to call his own, the Prince of Wales was ostensibly independent and free to do as he wished. But his life was circumscribed by both convention and the demands of his father, some of which were enshrined in law.

The Bill of Rights of 1689 and the Act of Settlement of 1701 together defined the relationship of the monarch to Parliament and the terms of succession to the throne. Although they drastically limited the powers of the monarch, kings were left with two active royal prerogatives, the right to declare war and the right to form and dismiss governments. In practice these prerogatives were usually exercised in conjunction with the executive; but their existence allowed the monarch to influence politics from behind the scenes and, occasionally, to act without the knowledge of Parliament. In 1772, for instance, George III, in concert with the prime minister, Lord North, ordered the secret mobilization of a huge fleet of thirty-two ships of the line to force the rescue of his imprisoned sister Queen Caroline Matilda from Kronborg Castle in Helsingør.

Opposition politicians were always suspicious of kings, and quick to sniff out 'secret influence', as it was called. Amazingly, George III's preparations for war with Denmark were kept hidden: the Danish government backed down when it heard of them and agreed to release his sister, their queen. The existence of the royal prerogatives, however, particularly in the domestic sphere, meant that monarchs could exert pressure on governments and, behind the scenes, favour particular politicians. Any Prince of Wales, setting himself up in opposition to his father, could do the same, making promises of future appointments and power. Politics then became a battleground on which family quarrels could be played out in public gestures.

Most of the time the king, who held the prerogative powers, had the upper hand, though the Prince of Wales could make his life very uncomfortable. Not surprisingly, given his low estimation of his eldest son, George III was keen to impose his authority as far as he could upon him, setting out several unwritten codes of behaviour that should accompany the Prince of Wales's majority and independence. First and most important, although the prince was of necessity allowed his own choice of companions, his own way of life and his own views, he should not stray so far into any political coterie as to threaten the king's government or the political stability of the nation. Second, he should stay within his income. Third, he should take care not to make himself a laughing stock or such an object of satire that the status of the monarchy was compromised or diminished.

To this list the king added three things that were absolutely forbidden. The prince could not travel abroad without the king's permission. He was forbidden from taking any active military role. Finally, he could not, under the terms of the Royal Marriages Act of 1772, marry without the king's permission before the age of twenty-five, or marry a divorced woman or a Roman Catholic, ever.

Already set against everything that his father stood for, the newly independent prince now had the means to defy him. In the decade between his coming of age and the outbreak of war with France in 1793, he flouted all the rules the king laid down, except that he was never able to get permission either to leave the country or to serve in any active military role, despite repeated attempts to do both. Even by Hanoverian standards, his rebellion was spectacular, and it was played out with a concomitant absence of affection and goodwill on both sides.

Long before he moved to Carlton House, the prince had discovered the pleasures of conviviality and cards (though he professed to like only games of chance), and found a ready abetter in his cheerful and dissolute uncle, Prince Henry, Duke of Cumberland. Estranged from the king since his secret marriage to a rakish widow, Mrs Horton, Cumberland set up a slapdash household in Cumberland House in Pall Mall. In Cumberland House, the Prince of Wales was able to get drunk, meet actresses and sing bawdy songs. Pretty soon he found a circle of companions who not only led him cheerfully into all sorts of fun, but also introduced him to politics. So now that he had a household of his own, the prince was able to add to his father's discomfort by setting himself up in political opposition.

Inevitably the prince gravitated towards just those politicians that George III disliked most, the set of radical Whigs and their supporters. These Whigs noisily sided with the American colonists in the Revolutionary War, attacked the crown at every opportunity, sought to limit the royal prerogatives and appealed for support directly to under-represented and restless urban voters. Their undisputed leader was the brilliant, charismatic and corpulent Charles James Fox, who had burst on to the political scene by dazzling the House of Commons with his eloquence when first elected an MP in 1768 at the age of nineteen.

The prince was entranced by Fox and in the early 1780s enthusiastically joined his friends and drinking companions in Brooks's Club, at Newmarket and at Fox's grimy lodgings in St James's Street, where Fox entertained in a state of dishevelled undress, his chin unshaven and his hairy chest prominent beneath an old and dirty nightgown. Fox was more than a brilliant raconteur. He had deeply held beliefs in social and religious tolerance and political amelioration; but his political recklessness scuppered his chances of effecting real change. By 1784 his lack of strategic judgement had condemned him to a life on the backbenches and a role as a figurehead for such causes as the abolition of slavery, religious toleration and the extension of the franchise, which carried immense importance in the long term but were beyond the daily power struggles in the Houses of Parliament.

Fox was less a rebel than someone who had no interest in convention, protocol or rank. He ended his life in a modest suburban villa, having refused to take a title, content simply to be himself. He married a courtesan of obscure origins, Elizabeth Armitstead, and retired without rancour to a life of cricket, reading and writing bits and pieces of history. In time, it would become obvious that Fox and the prince had little in common, but in the early 1780s they were united in their wish to taunt and discomfort both the king and the deeply unpopular government of Lord North, which in the eyes of many was intent on prolonging the pointless, wrong and destructive war in America.

Opposition politicians, with Fox prominent among them, energetically prosecuted the idea of the king's baleful influence on government and sought to advertise it in increasingly personal attacks. In 1780, at the height of the American Revolutionary War, the opposition launched a demand for greater scrutiny of crown pensions that were paid from the public coffers. This lightly veiled attack on the king allowed the MP John Dunning to bring the famous motion on 6 April that 'the influence of the crown has increased, is increasing, and ought to be diminished'.

The king took all this badly, and his sense of outrage increased after the surrender of the British army at Yorktown in October 1781 and the consequent fall of Lord North's government five months later. As the war dragged on and seamen and soldiers continued to die, the king's intransigence drew more and more opprobrium and his sense of persecution grew. In the turmoil after Lord North's resignation, when two administrations came and went in as many years, George III was finally forced to accept three successive governments in which Fox held prominent office, to the delight of the Prince of Wales. Peace was concluded with America in 1783. The king was humiliated and miserable. He even considered abdicating and retiring to Hanover, where he thought his subjects would be more grateful and deferential than either the Americans or his brothers and his sons.

Given the king's discomfort and deep unpopularity, a triumphant Prince of Wales might have thought that he had finally got the better of his father. Unexpectedly, however, events began to move the king's way. In 1784 the coalition government in which Fox was Secretary of State for Foreign Affairs was forced out of office. Fox was on the backbenches again, and was to remain there for almost two decades. The king appointed a new prime minister, the unforthcoming and austere William Pitt (the Younger), who stayed in power, with only a single break, until 1806.

With Fox out of office, Carlton House became more a louche palace of excess and filial rebellion than a truly threatening reversionary centre of power. Relations between the king and his heir, however, were as bad as ever. George III was damning about his son's extravagance. The prince, who had been spending vast sums that he did not have on the remodelling and decoration of Carlton House and its gardens, despised his father's frugality, writing: 'the King is grown so stingy with regard to himself [that] he will hardly allow himself 3 coats in a year.'[16] The king took the moral high ground, telling the prince loftily that he was merely 'an affectionate father trying to save his son from perdition'.[17] This tone further alienated the prince, who complained to his absent brother Frederick in the summer of 1784: 'his behaviour is so excessively unkind [that] there are moments when I can hardly ever put up with it. Sometimes not speaking to me when he sees me for three weeks together, & hardly ever at Court, speaking to people on each side of me & then missing me, & then if he does honour me with a word, 'tis either merely, "'tis very hot or very cold".'[18]

This dance of mutual dislike continued unabated throughout the 1780s, but the political differences between the king and his heir were gradually whittled away. This was partly because the king's popularity was slowly increasing and partly because the prince was too occupied by affairs of the heart and purse to concentrate on politics for long enough to do any real damage.

2

Growing and Living

The Prince of Wales grew up without any of the blushing self-consciousness his father had shown in his youth. Prince George was uninhibited and expressive in every way. A child of the age of sensibility, when feeling was taken as a sign of sincerity and tears were a quite acceptable accompaniment to joy or sadness, he was emotionally, physically and verbally unrestrained. Visitors were charmed by his unselfconscious affection. All his life he was kind to threatened and unthreatening creatures: animals, children and his unfortunate and often miserable sisters, with whom he sided and whom he frequently helped in their unequal battles with the king and queen to be allowed to lead lives of their own.

Once into his teens, the prince turned his roving eye on the women around him in the royal household. In 1779, at the age of sixteen, he fell in love with Lady Mary Hamilton, an assistant governess to his sisters. Never stopping to wonder whether she would welcome his attentions, he showered her with seventy-five letters in as many days, assuring her of his devotion and regretting that his rank prevented him from marrying her, at least for the present. Mary Hamilton was one of the few women recorded as refusing the prince's tumultuous advances. She did so not only because she was shrewd enough to see that the role of a mistress could never end well, but also because her piety and propriety forbade her from succumbing. Prince George registered only temporary regret. Pretty soon he was looking beyond the stultifying court and its virtuous dull courtiers to the much more exciting arenas of the theatres, clubs and racier drawing rooms of the city. There he found all the delicious amorous opportunities that money and rank could put his way.

In the second half of the eighteenth century, after the end of the European wars in 1763 and at the start of large-scale commercial exploitation of Britain's imperial possessions, money poured into London. The city quickly became the largest in Europe, a place of extravagance, poverty and constant change. After the Act of Settlement limited the power of the crown, political and financial power definitively passed from the court to the city. This, coupled with the fact that the press operated with a freedom and scope unparalleled anywhere else in the world, made London unique as a crucible of change and economic vitality.

Women, the objects of seduction, desire, scandal, poignancy and sympathy in a society where power and money overwhelmingly lay with men, offered some of the most valuable copy the press could find. The free press and the vibrant culture of theatre and display, backed by plenty of cash and a commitment to spend it, combined to produce the first fully fledged commercial culture of celebrity. Actresses and courtesans – who often doubled roles – became stars who could, if they were shrewd enough, rise up the social ranks, make a fortune and, in a few extraordinary cases, marry into the governing class. Those who flourished best were those who could operate without scruple, and live purely for social and commercial advantage. Those who mixed emotion, or even love, with the attention and excitement they were paid to provide, invariably suffered.

The Prince of Wales was keen to get into this glorious male playground as soon as he could after his failure with Mary Hamilton, and quickly fell for the actress Mary Robinson. He watched her playing Perdita in David Garrick's adaptation of *The Winter's Tale* at the Drury Lane Theatre in December 1779 and a few days later began to besiege her with letters, demands and declarations. He snipped off a lock of his hair and despatched it in an envelope on which he wrote 'to be redeemed'. He sent a miniature of himself. He suggested that she come to an assignation with him, dressed as a boy. They met. Mary Robinson recorded later how sweet and melodious his voice was, how great his charm. The prince promised her £20,000 as soon as he was twenty-one, which was four long years away. Mrs Robinson gave up her husband and her day job, and, for a few months, until George grew bored, she became his mistress. Crowds followed her about London. She spent money lavishly, running up debts of several thousands of pounds. The end came when the prince, having turned his attention to a Scottish adventuress and divorcée, Grace Dalrymple Elliott, abruptly wrote to her to say that they must 'meet no more'.[1]

Mrs Robinson held a good hand of cards in the form of the prince's letters and written promises of cash, and she played it well. She refused as 'insulting' an initial bid of £5,000 for the letters from the prince's advisers, and threatened to leave England and take them with her if a better offer was not forthcoming. Eventually she settled for the £5,000, an annuity of £500 a year and a legacy for her daughter of £250 a year. This was a hefty bill, and the prince had no way to settle it without involving his father. The king was predictably enraged and had to go cap in hand to the prime minister, Lord North, for the money. That this was a humiliating repeat of a request he had made a few years earlier on behalf of his scapegrace brother Prince Henry did not escape him, and it galled him the more since it was now in Henry's house that the Prince of Wales was carousing away his evenings.

The form of social and private life the prince enjoyed remained substantially the same throughout his life. He didn't hunt much, because he disliked killing animals, and though he was passionate about his stables and horses, he preferred to watch the racing rather than dashing about on horseback himself. His was an urban culture, even when the seaside charms of Brighton captured his imagination in the mid 1780s: a culture of street strolling, carriage driving, music, mimicry and drinking. In the wider society of the upper classes, the sexual segregation of pastimes increased, especially after the French Revolution, which in Britain killed off fashionable French mores. Though the Prince of Wales dallied in the male world of slumming and prize-fighting and in the clubs that flourished in Britain from the last quarter of the eighteenth century, he tended in his private life to stay true to aristocratic, and particularly Whig, drawing-room culture.

In this, as in many areas of his life, George followed habits that prevailed in Britain before the French Revolutionary

Wars of the 1790s. He was a child of the 1760s and 1770s in his habits and pleasures, despite being forbidden by his father from travelling on the continent, which meant that he missed an essential part of aristocratic education and, for many, a continued pleasure of life. This did not change even after the French Revolution. In the 1790s and first decade of the nineteenth century, when young men of the upper classes were developing and inhabiting an increasingly male social and professional world, and the influence of evangelical religion was making headway against the moral laxity of Enlightenment culture, George continued to enjoy mixed and jolly company. He disliked and never adopted the growing division of the day into work and leisure, preferring to scramble things up so that visitors might arrive as he (notionally) went through his accounts or saw to official business. Quite often, wrote the memoirist Nathaniel Wraxall, visitors found him in bed, no matter what the hour, 'rolling about from side to side in a state approaching to nudity', and from there, 'gave audience to his friends and received information of every sort; it constituted his throne, his cabinet, and his council-chamber'.[2] Both in the parlour and, in the evening, in the drawing room he always had mixed groups, and enjoyed the company of women, especially comfortable, older women who were complaisant and flattering and took the edge off his boredom.

The prince's method as a lover was to wear women down with staggeringly lengthy written declarations of his desires and needs. If these failed, or were tossed aside, he was sure to fall ill. He was subject to illness at times of emotional stress throughout his life, and was convinced that it usually started in the mind. In 1799, during a period of emotional strain, he wrote to his mother's adviser, Dr John Turton, 'Mine is a very nervous and so far a delicate fibre, consequently the disorders of the body in general with me owe their source to the mind.'[3] This connection struck seasoned observers, among them Charles James Fox's nephew Lord Holland, as self-serving. 'He generally, it seems, assailed the hearts which he wished to carry by exciting their commiserations for his sufferings and their apprehensions for his health,' Holland wrote wearily in 1806.[4]

Early in 1784, when he was twenty-one, the prince met Maria Fitzherbert, a twenty-seven-year-old Catholic, twice widowed and extremely devout. Attractive and pleasant-looking, with a warm air, deep brown eyes and the full figure that the prince was partial to, she instantly captured his attention when he spotted her at the opera. George declared his interest immediately, and talked incessantly of her beauty and his love for her. Maria was susceptible to his charm and flattered by the stream of gifts and invitations that he sent to her house in Park Street in Mayfair. She was often in his company and further endeared herself to him by showing herself a good listener and sympathetic to his many complaints. None the less, her piety was unwavering and she resisted all his advances.

George pressed on through the spring and early summer of 1784. Understanding that Maria had religious scruples, he declared that he wished to marry her. Mrs Fitzherbert was well aware that his promises were empty, however. Marriage to the Prince of Wales was forbidden by the terms of the Royal Marriages Act because George was under twenty-five and anyway could not marry without his father's permission. Beyond that, marriage would debar the prince from the throne, since, by the terms of the 1701 Act of Settlement, he could not marry a Catholic and inherit the crown.

By the summer of 1784, Mrs Fitzherbert was harassed and worn out. She declared her intention to leave the country and stay abroad indefinitely. In response, the prince began to employ the most extreme of the tactics Lord Holland was to observe. First he fell ill and then on 8 July, the night before Mrs Fitzherbert was due to go, he stabbed himself in the chest (or, as another report suggested, he had been bled to relieve his high tension, and then ripped his bandages off to let the blood flow again). Mrs Fitzherbert was persuaded to come to his bedside in Carlton House, where she found him distraught, with blood still dripping from the fresh wound in his chest. Shocked by his condition, she promised to marry him, whereupon the prince was able to sit up in bed and slip a ring on her finger.

As soon as he had Mrs Fitzherbert's consent, the prince rallied a great deal and declared that he would very soon follow her to France. Before she left the next day, Mrs Fitzherbert wrote a deposition saying that a promise of marriage extracted in such a way was worthless. None the less her agreement placed her under some emotional obligation and, just as importantly, gave the prince the excuse to bombard her with letters.

The moment Mrs Fitzherbert had gone, the prince applied to the king for permission to go abroad, citing his need to economize as the reason. George III chose to take his son's explanation at face value, refusing to give him permission to travel, as a matter of course, but enthusiastically taking up the matter of the prince's vast and mounting debts, which were the result of the 'frivolous and irregular passion' that directed his conduct.[5] The prince had put his own head in this noose, and it only tightened in the following months. Pressing on, the king demanded to know the extent and nature of his son's debts. Reluctantly, the prince asked his treasurer, Colonel Hotham, for a list and tally to submit to the king. When the account was delivered, it showed that already, only a year after setting up his own household, the prince owed the vast sum of £147,000.

The prince left Hotham's list on his desk for several months, and by the time it was eventually sent to the king, in March 1785, he had lost interest in it. His only real concern, sitting there, was to write enormous letters to Maria Fitzherbert, who was drifting aimlessly about the continent, her resolve weakened by their almost daily arrival. It was a miserable half-life, as the prince knew very well. Eventually she wavered and gave some sort of assent to his entreaties. A final letter of forty-five pages arrived in France in mid November 1785, accompanied by a little painting of one of the prince's blue-grey eyes, spookily floating against an azure ground. He was not letting her out of his sight. In his letter, George gave Mrs Fitzherbert a long, undoubtedly specious explanation of why the king would connive at their marriage, and ended with his clarion call: 'Come then, oh! come, dearest of wives, best & most adored of women, come & for ever crown with bliss him who will thro' life endeavour to convince you by his love & attention of his wishes to be [the] best of husbands & who will ever remain unto [the] latest moments of his existence, *unalterably thine.*[6]

Maria came back. The two were married on 15 December 1785 by a clergyman sprung from debtors' prison for the purpose and rewarded not just by the payment of his immediate debts of £500, but by his appointment as a chaplain to the prince, and the promise of a bishopric when George succeeded to the throne. Under canon law and, all-importantly for Maria, in the eyes of the Catholic Church, the marriage was valid; but under English law it was not – a happy situation for the prince, who could thus both have a wife and not have one. Maria, at least, had saved her immortal soul.

So things went on contentedly for a couple of years, the prince in Carlton House, Mrs Fitzherbert, as she continued to be called, in a grand residence round the corner in Pall Mall. They spent most days and evenings, if not nights, together. Despite numerous rumours, it seems unlikely that they had any children, though claims were made at various times that children who lived with them, or with Mrs Fitzherbert alone, were theirs, especially a boy called James Ord and a girl, Mary Anne Smythe, whom Mrs Fitzherbert described as her adopted niece. Mary Anne married the younger son of a peer, a marriage that might lend support to the idea that she was the prince's daughter. But no real evidence of children appears in what remains of Mrs Fitzherbert's archive, or elsewhere.

The prince's new domesticity, together with the splendour of Mrs Fitzherbert's house, which was redecorated at a cost of £50,000, inevitably led to intense speculation about a possible marriage and to increasing pressure on George's finances. By mid 1786, he was petitioning his father again to come to his aid, adding insult to the injury of Colonel Hotham's list, which he had simply disregarded. The king continued to address his son with lofty disdain, using his annoying tactic of addressing the Prince of Wales in the third person, to emphasize the moral distance between them: 'From everything which has passed between me and the Prince of Wales during these last two years, relative to his embarrassed situation, he must have seen that I hold it impossible even to enter on the consideration of any means to relieve him untill I should receive a sufficient explanation of his past expences, and see a prospect of reasonable security against a continuation of his extravagance.'[7]

Perhaps the prince did try to economize for a while, at least moving out of London during the summer, which might have suggested a drop in his expenses. In 1786 he took the lease of the house in Brighton that would eventually become the Royal Pavilion. He established Mrs Fitzherbert in a villa nearby and passed the time in quiet seaside pursuits. But by the spring of the following year his finances had not improved and he determined to bypass the king and go directly to Parliament in search of redress. Since his Whig friends were unwilling to raise the issue in Parliament, knowing that it would draw with it questions as to whether the prince was married to a Catholic, which would be disastrous for the opposition cause, George turned to an independent MP who was prepared to bring a motion for relief of his finances to the House. But as soon as this was done, it predictably brought with it the question of the prince's constitutional status, and thus the question of his marriage. George denied to Fox that he was married and Fox repeated his denial to the House of Commons in good faith, saying that he had His Royal Highness's 'direct authority' for his statement.[8]

Fox's emphatic declaration had the required effect. In the spring of 1787 Parliament voted the prince £161,000 to pay his debts, along with £60,000 to finish Carlton House, and the king added another £10,000 a year to his son's income from the Civil List. However, when Fox learned that he had been misled, his relationship with the prince, already strained because of Mrs Fitzherbert's dislike of him, began to falter. The extraordinary events of the following few years eroded it further. By the early 1790s, the opposition had lost all hope that the prince might support it, or bring it into government should he accede to power.

In October 1788, George III suffered a recurrence of the severe stomach pain and breathing difficulties that he had suffered in 1765 and again in 1787. This time, however, he did not recover after a few days, as he had before. His illness grew rapidly worse, with continued stomach pains, swollen feet, yellow eyes and brown urine. These symptoms were accompanied by acute mental disturbance, constant, rapid talking, hallucinations and the utmost misery. A stream of doctors came and went, baffled and terrified. The king could find no solace in music, and his vision began to go. One day he burst into tears and cried out that 'He wished to God he might die, for he was going to be mad.'[9]

The exact nature of George III's illness may never be known. Regarded as madness at the time, it was retrospectively diagnosed as an organic disease, porphyria, by

Ida Macalpine and Richard Hunter in 1969.[10] Although Hunter and Macalpine were psychiatrists rather than experts in porphyria or any other organic disease, this diagnosis was seized on by those who regarded mental illness as a stigma that cast a taint on the royal family. It was widely accepted for half a century, but recently the pendulum has swung back towards a diagnosis of bipolar disorder. The diagnosis is immaterial. The effects of physical and mental illness could not and cannot be separated; the king was both ill and mad.

During the next three months, a period which came to be known as the Regency Crisis, Parliament struggled as much as the king's doctors with the consequences of his illness and with his complete inability to carry out his duties. In such circumstances it was accepted that a regent who had full royal powers had to be installed. That of course meant the Prince of Wales, who was the last person the prime minister, William Pitt, wanted. By November 1788, Pitt could no longer put off the issue. Despite his popularity in the country, the prime minister was a fairly isolated figure, personally disliked by those around him. He could not count on a parliamentary majority. Once he became Regent, the Prince of Wales would acquire the royal prerogative to dismiss and form governments, and it was widely assumed that he would dismiss Pitt and bring in the opposition, with Fox at its head.

Given Mrs Fitzherbert's dislike of Fox and the prince's subsequent political behaviour, this assumption may have been over-optimistic on the opposition's part. Pitt skilfully stalled for time by adjourning Parliament on 20 November. When it reassembled in December, Fox overplayed his hand in the House of Commons debate, declaring that the prince had the same right to assume royal powers as he would if the king were dead, a position that shocked Parliament and was condemned by much of the press as unconstitutional. The debate dragged on, and Pitt succeeded in getting sufficient restrictions placed on any regency to make it likely that he would remain in power. On 12 February 1789, the Regency Bill passed the Commons and went up to the Lords. At that very moment, to the astonishment of his family, George III was declared by his doctors to be 'in a progressive state of amendment'.[11] In the following days he began to recover. Pitt survived, and went on to head the Tory administration until February 1801. The opposition had lost its chance.

The king was weakened and submissive after his ordeal, and wept piteously when the Prince of Wales, accompanied by his brother Frederick, Duke of York, arrived at Kew to see him on 23 February 1789. Queen Charlotte, however, was implacably angry that her son had allowed Parliament to debate the question of the king's illness. She did not know that drafts of a speech accepting a regency had already been written when the king began to recover. Had she done so she might never have forgiven her son. As it was, numerous slights of protocol were directed towards the Prince of Wales and his brother Frederick. They retaliated by petulant acts of family disobedience: talking loudly throughout the service of thanksgiving for the king's recovery in April, and ostentatiously absorbing themselves in pleasure and dissipation. It did the Prince of Wales no good, and his behaviour dragged the opposition down with him.

In the long battle between father and son, the king was now definitely on top. His illness and frailty, and the humility with which he accepted them, endeared him greatly to the public. George III was more popular than he had been since his accession, while the prince was regarded as a loose-living sybarite, careless in his life and his friends and unfeeling towards his own father.

Partly to get away from his family, partly as an exercise in damage limitation, the Prince of Wales and the Duke of York left London and travelled up to the north of England, where they stayed at Wentworth Woodhouse and then Castle Howard as guests of Lord Fitzwilliam and the Earl of Carlisle respectively. Despite the prominence of Fitzwilliam and Carlisle in Whig circles, Prince George 'was properly attentive & civil to those who were adverse in their politicks, so as rather to please than to offend them', Edmund Burke wrote approvingly to the prince's equerry, Captain Payne.[12] *The Times* reported that he garnered 'great affection from all ranks of people' wherever he went.[13]

This change in sentiment was only temporary. Back in London, the prince was once again sidelined and shunned at Windsor and Kew and pilloried in the press for womanizing and drunkenness. Now described equivocally in *The Times* as a man 'who at all times would prefer a girl and a bottle, to politics and a sermon', he gave his critics plenty of evidence for his profligacy. Drunk at Boodle's club, hauled out of Ranelagh Gardens for misbehaviour, widely rumoured to be married as well as womanizing, hanging out with reprobates whose escapades filled the newspapers, accused of rigging the odds at Newmarket, arriving hours late for his own levees and dinners at Carlton House: it was at this time that the caricaturist James Gillray portrayed him splayed out drunk after dinner in *A Voluptuary under the Horrors of Digestion*. In this famous print, published in 1792, the prince's immense stomach fills the centre of the picture, as he leans back, waistcoat unbuttoned and bursting, and picks his teeth with a fork. In obvious contrast to Gillray's depictions of the king and queen as austere and parsimonious, if familial and loving, the prince is alone and degraded. Decanters and a wine glass stand on one side, an overflowing chamber pot and a cascade of bills on the other, and empty wine bottles lie scattered under the chair. The prince stares defiantly out of the picture, much as he must have tried to face down his father's disapproval.

Relations between the Prince of Wales and his father did not improve. The king could find no way to love his heir, and had no pressing need to do so. The mood in the country was on his side. The French Revolution, which began a few months after the king's illness, quickly engendered an upsurge in patriotism, and a respect for both the monarchy and the dutiful, austere, self-regulated and uncomplaining way of life that George III exemplified.

The Revolution, and then the long war against France, which would last for nearly two decades, resulted in a intense hostility to what were seen as loose French-style morals and compounded the backlash against the prince. A new kind of British masculinity was formed in these years, which in the following decades would be solidified in the forges of empire and in the notion of service to monarch and country. Despite his intelligence, generosity and charm, the Prince of Wales was a poor avatar for this emerging form of Britishness. He represented its opposite; his father, who had declared in his first speech to Parliament that he 'gloried in the name of Briton', was discovered to embody it already.

Few reactions of the Prince of Wales to the early years of the French Revolution survive. Charles James Fox had welcomed the outbreak of the Revolution by declaring, 'How much the greatest event it is that ever happened in the world! and how much the best!'[14] In his maiden speech to the House of Lords in May 1792, the prince spoke against increasing censorship of the press and a proclamation against seditious writings; but his mood hardened with that of the country and the government after the imprisonment of the French royal family, the September Massacres and the abolition of the French monarchy on 21 September 1792. When news of Louis XVI's execution on 21 January 1793 reached the prince, the full implications of the Revolution for his own family and what he described a few months later as 'THE VERY EXISTANCE OF EVERY PRINCE AT THIS MOMENT' hit home.[15] The next day he wrote to his mother: 'I am not equal to meeting any of you this evening, overpowered with the shocking & horrid events of France.'[16]

After war was declared on Britain by France on 1 February 1793, the prince followed its course avidly, but his hopes of being allowed to serve in the army in anything more than a ceremonial capacity were soon dashed. The rapprochement with his parents occasioned by the guillotining of

Louis XVI was little more than skin deep, and he had to follow the great events of the next twenty years from the sidelines. The change in his domestic political affiliation, however, was soon evident. He became an unashamed supporter of the Tory government. He turned against abolition of the slave trade (and thus irretrievably against Fox), heartily endorsing a speech in the House of Lords that attacked the abolitionist politician William Wilberforce, and began to measure politics against a single standard: whether it was, in his opinion, for or against monarchical principles.[17]

Despite the prince's new approbation of the austere William Pitt, his own private behaviour changed little in the years between the Regency Crisis and the mid 1790s. His debts rose inexorably, to almost £630,000. His relationship with Mrs Fitzherbert became rocky and fractured. After five or six years, the eye which he had sent her painted and encased in gold when she was in France had begun to wander. It settled, after a couple of adventures, on the actress Anna Maria Crouch, who had come into fame acting Polly Peachum in *The Beggar's Opera*. This was a role that had form. Half a century earlier, the original Polly, Lavinia Fenton, had parlayed her stage role as the moll of the dashing highwayman Macheath into the altogether more solid position as the mistress and then wife of the Duke of Bolton. Perhaps fancying himself as another Macheath surrounded by adoring women, the prince pursued Anna Maria enthusiastically. Astutely, she negotiated, and received a very large fee before her surrender. Gossip had it that she made £10,000 on the deal, and that the prince, in the end, slept with her only once.

Mrs Fitzherbert could and did forgive the prince his dalliances. Things were patched up; but greater difficulty arrived in 1793 in the shape of the Countess of Jersey, an experienced and older woman who was closer to the prince's day-to-day life.

Lady Jersey was in her early forties and married with nine children. She knew the ways of the court, where her elderly husband had held various positions. The memoirist Nathaniel Wraxall described her as a woman of 'irresistible seduction and fascination'.[18] It was soon clear that she was more than a match for Mrs Fitzherbert, who had none of her controlling allure and was unable to keep her temper when hurt. The prince was in the mood for change and wanted to be told what to do. He seized on Lady Jersey's suggestion that Mrs Fitzherbert was the cause of his unpopularity. Without her, Lady Jersey pointed out, he would easily be able to get rid his massive debts: all he had to do was declare publicly his intention of getting married.

After some hesitation, the prince agreed. He wrote two letters to Mrs Fitzherbert on the same day in June 1794. The first began with an evasive formula, 'My dear love, I have just receiv'd a letter from my sister by the coach this evening, desiring me to come to Windsor, which . . .' He signed off, 'Adieu, my dear love, excuse haste, Ever thine', but followed this with a blunt message saying that he would never enter her house again. Mrs Fitzherbert wrote on the prince's second letter, 'Lady Jersey's influence', and left Brighton immediately.[19]

The prince professed his misery at this unreasonable behaviour. 'I really think myself too ill used,' he wrote to his equerry Captain Payne in July, adding: 'God knows what I have done to merit it';[20] but the break allowed him, a month later, to go to the king and declare his intention of what George III declared 'a more creditable line of life' – that is, to get married.[21] He had even chosen a bride, his first cousin, twenty-six-year-old Princess Caroline of Brunswick.

3
Loving and Hating

Although, in 1791, the Prince of Wales had declared to his brother Frederick that he would never marry unless 'I preferr'd the woman I was going to marry to every creature existing in the world, and knew enough of the disposition of my wife to think it would form the happiness and not the misery of my future days', three years later he disregarded this certain self-knowledge entirely.[1] As soon as he had decided to get married publicly and legally, George made a hasty choice and settled on a bride without either the customary half-disguised diplomatic visit of scrutiny or, apparently, any serious preliminary research at all.

If it occurred to the prince that Caroline of Brunswick was a human being he would have to live with, talk to and behave well towards, rather than an overdraft reduction scheme and the means of delivering an heir, he did not show it. Contempt, blame and self-pity were the emotions that predominated in his conduct from the moment he decided to get married and throughout the debacle of his marriage itself. His vaunted condescension, kindness and charm were very rarely in evidence.

Just how the prince settled on Princess Caroline from among the available European Protestant princesses is not clear. Certainly his mother and father had nothing to do with it: the prince announced his choice at the same time as his intention. The king was delighted at an alliance of cousins, calling it 'the only proper alliance',[2] but the queen was horrified, convinced by her own enquiries that Caroline was lewd and indecent. Writing to her brother Charles, she described Caroline as 'a woman I do not recommend at all'.[3]

Surprisingly, it took four months after the prince's announcement of his choice before his envoy James Harris arrived in Brunswick to make the formal request for Princess Caroline's hand. Harris was a seasoned diplomat and a man who knew Prince George well. From the moment he saw Princess Caroline, he was filled with foreboding. She was small, plump, full-chested and fair-haired, but neither pretty nor complaisant in the manner that attracted the prince. Over the next few days, Harris became progressively more horrified at her behaviour: she was from their first meeting boisterous, uninhibited and outspoken. She had little time for etiquette and revelled in flirting, dancing and intimate revelations.

Harris, however, was a diplomat who stuck to his brief. He was not required to report any of this, to advise the prince against his choice or to take steps to school the princess in how she would be required to behave when she was married to the heir to the throne of Great Britain. His instructions were simply to demand Caroline's hand and escort her to London. None the less, he attempted to tell the princess what might be in store, strenuously recommending 'perfect silence on *all* subjects for six months after her arrival' and an approach to the prince that had 'softness, enduring, and caresses' at its heart.[4]

Caroline knew that she could not expect fidelity from the prince, and cheerfully told Harris that she was 'determined never to appear jealous', but her impetuosity boded ill.[5] The prince was not going to alter his way of life: a tranquil marriage would depend on how he was managed. Exactly the same could be said of Caroline, but the onus was all on her. A prince could behave as he wished; his wife must behave as was expected of her. This double standard, which was simply a magnification of wider mores, was inherent in the arrangement. Of Princess Caroline and Prince George, only one was obliged to change.

Caroline was ill-equipped to endure loneliness and lacked the ability to anticipate or plan for the long term. Harris noted in his diary, 'On summing up Princess Caroline's character to-day', that she had 'no judgment' and was 'caught by the first impression, led by the first impulse . . . loving to talk, and prone to confide'. Harris knew that the prince would dislike Caroline's disregard for etiquette and would make no effort to get her impulsiveness under control. 'In short,' he concluded gloomily, 'the Princess in the hands of a steady and sensible man would probably turn out well, but where it is likely she will find faults perfectly analogous to her own, she will fail.'[6]

On the boat over to Britain, Harris had to entreat Caroline to wash *'all over'*, explaining that the prince was 'very delicate' and would expect 'a long and very careful *toilette de propreté'.*[7] Washed and well dressed, Caroline arrived at Greenwich on 5 April 1795. Her escort to St James's Palace turned out to be none other than Lady Jersey, who had been appointed her lady-in-waiting and whom she already knew to be the prince's mistress.

At the palace, Caroline waited with Harris for the prince to appear. When he eventually came into the room, George took a look at his bride-to-be, who had followed Harris's advice and was attempting to kneel before him, 'raised her (gracefully enough), and embraced her'. Then, after a few words, he turned round, retreated to a far corner of the room and said to Harris, 'I am not well; pray get me a glass of brandy.' Harris demurred, saying, 'Sir, had you not better have a glass of water?' The prince lost his temper and left the room, saying, 'No; I will go directly to the Queen.'[8] Poor Caroline was left alone and told Harris in humiliated retaliation that the prince was very fat and not nearly as handsome as his portrait had suggested.

From this very bad start, things grew quickly worse. The prince was so drunk at the wedding on 8 April that he had to be helped into the Chapel Royal, and seemed on the point of tears throughout the ceremony. Report had it that he spent the wedding night collapsed in the fireplace, only climbing into bed with his bride in the morning. The prince told Harris that at that point Caroline had said, '*Ah mon dieu qu'il est gros!*', which convinced him that she was not a virgin because 'how should she know this without a previous means of comparison'?[9]

Luckily, the princess was obviously pregnant by the last week in June. The prince claimed to have been repelled by his wife's uncleanliness and only to have slept with her three times. Her pregnancy not only released him from the marital bed, but also delighted Queen Charlotte. For a while relations between the prince and his mother were warmer and closer as a result.

Indeed, from the time of his marriage, the prince's running battles with his parents, and particularly with the king, sometimes now dropped into the background. Although the prince's feud with his father remained a central drama of his family life, it was now joined, and often superseded, by his growing hatred of his wife. The impulsive decision to marry turned into a long nightmare of rage and regret in which both husband and wife lost standing, happiness and tranquillity.

From the start, however, Princess Caroline had the support of the public, which had scant regard for a prince whose reputation was already low. As the veteran politician Lord Melbourne explained years later to a curious young Queen Victoria, 'whatever she did, had no weight with the people, for, they said, it was all his fault at first . . . The way in which he treated her immediately after the marriage was beyond everything wrong and foolish. Considering the way *he lived* himself . . . he should never have attacked *her* character.'[10]

The marriage of the Prince of Wales took place against a background of political upheaval and unrest, and the actions of the prince and princess thus inevitably acquired a political resonance in the country, as Melbourne was aware. Although George sided increasingly with the anti-Jacobin government, and thus with his father's political stance, he was still castigated in cartoons and the press, while Caroline was taken up as a figurehead for populist anger against a corrupt governing class.

In a larger context also, the discord within the prince's marriage was mirrored in the instability of the wider world. The long wars with France and its allies formed the background to the drama of his marriage, to George III's recurring illness and finally to the Regency in 1811. The first round of hostilities was well under way by the time Britain joined the Austrians and Prussians fighting France in 1793, and the wars soon grew into a struggle for supremacy that spread beyond Europe into Africa and the Americas. After ten years of fighting there was a brief pause for breath, but the conflict resumed, and carried on until the defeat of Napoleon at the Battle of Waterloo, the subsequent dismembering of the Napoleonic empire and the restoration of Europe's royal families. The wars were a rumbling threat to the stability of the British state and monarchy. It was a threat that came and went, and it was exploited for repressive purposes, especially in the 1790s, by Pitt's regime; but it was only conclusively ended in 1815.

Apart from triggering this long, draining conflict, the triumph of republicanism in France had its echoes in small republican and anti-monarchical movements in Britain and in demands in Ireland for the establishment of a sovereign, independent republic. In Britain, groups that demanded and debated democratic change, such as the London Corresponding Society and its provincial branches, were targeted by spies and increasingly shut down by legislation that criminalized seditious meetings and publications. In Ireland, the Society of United Irishmen, an ecumenical republican society, was forced underground by 1794. Thereafter it turned away from attempts to reform the relationship between Ireland and Britain and became an armed movement for independence that eventually exploded in the unsuccessful Irish Rebellion of 1798 and had its consequence in the union with Great Britain in 1801.

Despite this febrile political atmosphere, in which monarchists and the Pitt government consolidated their power by legislative and draconian means, the British economy flourished until war really took its toll in the second decade of the nineteenth century. Demands for greater democracy and for other radical and evangelical causes such as the end of the slave trade, universal male suffrage and the rights of women went hand in hand with enormous economic expansion. Growth was particularly evident in London, in port cities such as Liverpool, Bristol and Glasgow, and in the industrial heartlands of Birmingham, Manchester, Yorkshire and the Potteries. It was fuelled by fast technical innovation, infrastructural investments in road and canal building and huge amounts of money from imperial exploitation and expanding markets. In the second half of the eighteenth century, the populations of Birmingham, Manchester, Glasgow and the Yorkshire mill towns grew extremely quickly. Wealth from the empire, particularly the Caribbean and India, fuelled a building boom in British cities and on large country estates. The face, the manners, the economy and the temper of the nation were also all changing fast, and would change again in the economic and industrial crisis after Waterloo that culminated in the Peterloo Massacre of 1819.

In the years between the birth of the Prince of Wales in 1762 and the beginning of his reign as George IV in 1820, the British Empire expanded dramatically. In 1757 the East India Company's victory at the Battle of Plassey began the violent and lucrative subordination of India. Soon afterwards the French and Dutch were all but run out of the subcontinent, leaving it open to British domination. This triumph was underlined by the Treaty of Paris of 1763, which ended the Seven Years War and finally delivered France's North American holdings into British hands. The loss of the American colonies in 1783 was a setback to Britain's imperial ambition, but this reverse was cancelled out by new gains in India and the Far East. With the exception of China, Britain was by the 1820s the fastest-growing and most commercially successful nation in the world.

This staggering change was surely the concern of the Prince of Wales, and must have repeatedly come into his official business. Yet the prince's surviving correspondence shows little interest in the commercial or intellectual issues of the day, with the notable exception of Catholic emancipation. In the decade after his marriage, the wars with France, in which several of his brothers were involved, and upon which the survival of the monarchy depended, did of course impinge upon him, as did the possibility of political change. He followed the progress of the wars, and his brothers' movements, but neither his correspondence nor the recollections of those who knew him suggest that his interests went much beyond the day-to-day. Although his archive is necessarily incomplete and much personal correspondence must be lost or is unavailable, George's published letters contain little evidence that he read anything much in philosophy, in the growing and fashionable area of political economy, in arguments for or against the slave trade, or in any other subject that commanded intellectual attention.

The exception was Catholic emancipation. The topic was a litmus test of progressive opinion in Britain in the second half of the eighteenth century, a cornerstone of Foxite Whig philosophy and a personal issue for the prince, because Maria Fitzherbert was a devout and practising Catholic. In 1797, two months after the French government had managed to send a fleet to Ireland in an abortive invasion attempt, the prince wrote a long memo to William Pitt, proposing that all '*restriction* and *disqualification*' be immediately removed from Irish Catholics in order to bind them to the British government and split the Irish republican movement.[11]

Although such a proposal did not amount to a demand for emancipation for British Catholics, since Ireland was until 1801 a separate, vassal, state, it conceded a principle that might be applied on the other side of the Irish Sea. The prince followed this sensible, if unworkable, suggestion with another one that was far less sensible: a declaration of his own 'wish and readiness to undertake the Government of Ireland, great and arduous as the task appears under the present circumstances'.[12] Pitt prudently declined to engage with this, or with the barrage of documents that followed it, simply passing everything on to the king. He was confident the king would do his job for him, and he was not mistaken. George III gave the proposal short shrift, both as a matter of principle, and because it came from his son. Reporting this to the prince's envoy, Pitt added with lofty disdain: 'his Majesty could not help apprehending that his Royal Highness suffering his name to be mixed in any discussions respecting political questions in that country was not likely to be productive of any beneficial effect.'[13] At this time of threat to the crown and the government both on the mainland and in Ireland, the prince had no public role to play, and this both his father and the prime minister were happy to point out.

Nine months almost to the day after the Prince and Princess of Wales were married, on 7 January 1796, Caroline gave birth to 'an *immense girl*', as the prince put it.[14] She was named Charlotte, and the king and queen were delighted. George III, congratulating his son, added pointedly: 'You are both young and I trust will have many children, and this newcomer will equally call for the protection of its parents and consequently be a bond of additional union.'[15] The prince, though, was far from thinking about additional union: his dynastic duty accomplished, he had no intention of adding to his family, or spending any time in his wife's company, let alone ever sleeping with her again.

The prince put this to his wife and at first Caroline agreed with the idea. George wrote to her on 30 April confirming that he would never, 'even in the event of an accident happening to my daughter . . . infringe the terms of the restriction by proposing, at any period, a connexion of a more particular nature'.[16] But the truce did not last long. Caroline soon became sad, then rebellious. The prince became petty, then vindictive. He demanded a separation. A slanging match broke out that continued for a year.

The king at first refused to grant a separation. He told

the prince that his marriage was not a mere private affair, but a 'public act', in which Parliament and the country were concerned.[17] The public was certainly not on the prince's side, and Parliament might take money for the princess out of her husband's Civil List income. While this threat might have delayed the outcome, it did not stop it. In the summer of 1797, Caroline was allowed to remove herself to a villa at Blackheath, and, temporarily at least, take Princess Charlotte with her.

As soon as his daughter was born, the prince's thoughts turned back to Mrs Fitzherbert. It was Maria who was '*the beloved & adored wife of my heart & soul*', and he wanted her back.[18] Lady Jersey was eventually despatched, and the prince concentrated on bringing Mrs Fitzherbert round in the same way that he had at the beginning of their relationship, bombarding her with letters, emissaries and gifts, including a bracelet engraved with the words '*Rejoindre ou mourir*'.[19] By the summer of 1799, Mrs Fitzherbert was so worn down that she agreed to consult the pope on the status of her marriage. The answer was favourable: in the eyes of the Catholic Church she and the prince were man and wife. The prince was delighted, declaring Catholicism the 'only religion for a gentleman'.[20] By the summer of 1800 the two were decisively back together, Mrs Fitzherbert making a public declaration of her reinstatement with a party in the gardens of her house with bands, marquees and entertainment from early afternoon until daylight the next day.[21]

This new phase of the relationship lasted until 1807, when the prince took up with Lady Hertford, and his long dependence on Maria Fitzherbert began to fray, ending in a final separation two years later. Despite George's reported dalliances with a dancer, Louise Hillisberg, with the notorious and successful courtesan Harriette Wilson and with two Frenchwomen, the Countess of Massereene and a certain Madame de Meyer, and despite the births of several natural children, his relationship with Mrs Fitzherbert was for the most part tranquil and happy. These years – when his spending continued unabated and domestic happiness took the edge off the prince's multiple grievances and his lack of anything to give him public purpose – brought out his best qualities: his kindness, charm, generosity and sense of fun.

Much time was spent at Brighton, where the Marine Pavilion, originally designed by Henry Holland, was expanded over the years by Holland's assistant Peter Frederick Robinson. A grand new house was built for Mrs Fitzherbert close by, rumoured to be connected to the Pavilion by an underground passage. The pace of life when the prince was in Brighton was relaxed, with long, excellent dinners, singing, late rising and sauntering on the Steine, as the seafront was called. The prince drank less during these years, or at least he was not so often blind drunk, though his size grew relentlessly. Mrs Fitzherbert also filled out, though she remained attractive, despite an ill-fitting set of false teeth.

After years of fear for the survival of the European monarchies, and his consequent support of repressive measures and Pitt's government, the prince's preference for the lackadaisical and fun-loving over the tense and austere gradually returned. It helped that after the Battle of Trafalgar in 1805 the fortunes of war turned against the French. Old

Whig friends, such as the playwright Richard Brinsley Sheridan and Lord and Lady Holland, and young ones such as Thomas Creevey, became social fixtures again. When William Pitt died of alcoholism in 1806 and the so-called Ministry of all the Talents was formed, with Lord Grenville as prime minister, several of the prince's Whig friends, including Lord Grey, Lord Fitzwilliam and the Earl of Moira, as well as Fox himself, came into office.

The happy political situation was very short-lived, however. Fox died in September the same year. The ministry managed to pass the bill for the abolition of the slave trade that Fox had proposed to the House, which became law in 1807, but further reform proved impossible. George III refused to sanction a proposal to allow Roman Catholics to serve in the militia, a precursor for the looming debate on Catholic emancipation, and the prince did nothing to stop the government's subsequent collapse and fall, despite the presence of his friends. He told Lord Moira that he had 'ceased to be a party man' with Fox's death, but the truth was that, though he might continue to see Whigs as friends, he had been spooked by the French Revolution and the execution of Louis XVI.[22] By 1807 he had little left politically in common with his Whig friends, and would progressively abandon even his formerly staunch support for Catholic emancipation.

In Brighton, and at times in Carlton House, the prince forgot all this. He delighted in sociable visitors and particularly in children. In the autumn of 1800, Mrs Fitzherbert began to take care of a toddler, Mary Seymour, whose ailing mother, Lady Horatia Seymour, had been advised to leave Britain for the warmth of Madeira, where she died in July 1801. Her husband died a few weeks afterwards, leaving Mary, or Minny as she was always called, an orphan in Mrs Fitzherbert's care.

Minny was a lively and charming child and quickly became the daughter that Mrs Fitzherbert had never had. The prince was also devoted to her, and not only showered her with presents, but loved having her about, sitting her on his knee and chatting cheerfully to her. Everything continued harmoniously until 1804, when Minny's Seymour relatives began to object to the arrangement and demanded that she be returned to their care, as her father's will had implicitly stipulated. Mrs Fitzherbert was distraught. The prince declared that Minny's dying mother had asked him to be 'the father and protector through life, of this dear child'.[23] Her relatives denied any knowledge of this.

The case soon went to court, and Lord Eldon, the Lord Chancellor, found in the family's favour. Thomas Erskine, Mrs Fitzherbert's lawyer, advocated an appeal to the House of Lords, and, handily, had himself become Lord Chancellor by the time the appeal was heard. The prince and Mrs Fitzherbert also had the support of Minny's uncle and aunt, Lord and Lady Hertford, who proposed to take on the guardianship of their niece provided that they were allowed to do as they felt best for her. George canvassed the Lords energetically and a large majority found against the Seymours and in the Hertfords' favour. Not surprisingly, Lord and Lady Hertford immediately asked Mrs Fitzherbert to continue to care for their niece, an outcome that may have been rigged but ensured that Minny stayed happily where she was.

The commitment the Prince of Wales showed towards Minny Seymour was in growing contrast to his thinning relationship with his own daughter, Princess Charlotte, which was never free from shadows cast by the quarrels with his wife and his father. From the age of nine, Princess Charlotte lived at Warwick House, an unpretentious London townhouse across a narrow lane from Carlton House, going to Blackheath to see her mother, Windsor to see her grandparents and Weymouth with the royal party in the summer. She was an intelligent and chatty girl, surrounded by the adults who looked after and taught her, but bereft of company her own age. She spoke and read early. At eighteen months, she exclaimed cheerfully after her hair was cut, 'it all gone.' Each night at bedtime she declared, 'Bless papa, mama, Charlotte & friends', and a year later had mastered 'God Save the King' and the patriotic song 'Hearts of Oak'.[24]

Princess Charlotte's education turned out to be patchy, despite a rigorous programme drawn up for it. She developed a good knowledge of British history and liked novels, music, fun and pranks. She was an excellent linguist, although her German was poor, which distressed her grandmother, who would have liked to continue the family tradition of speaking German in private. Despite her physical proximity to her father, she saw little of him, and he rarely invited her to Carlton House, especially if, as happened increasingly as the years went on, he considered that she was showing a preference for her mother. Indeed, Princess Charlotte's childhood was dominated by the quarrel between the Prince and Princess of Wales, and when she began to show signs of independence, anger and unpredictable moods, the prince became convinced that she had inherited these characteristics from his wife, and neglected her because of it.

The king, however, doted on his granddaughter, and, as part of his own quarrel with his son, often invited her to visit him and the queen, sometimes pointedly extending the invitation to the Princess of Wales. Thus the maelstrom of family disunity and dislike whirled ever faster. The Princess of Wales tried to shore up her position by staying close to the king. The king, delighted by babies and seeking a role in the upbringing of the future queen, pointedly met the Princess of Wales and Princess Charlotte when the Prince of Wales wasn't there. The queen inevitably sided with the king, though she disliked the Princess of Wales and tried to remain on some sort of terms with her son. The Prince of Wales felt isolated by his parents, enraged with his wife and increasingly detached from his daughter.

After Princess Charlotte was removed from her care in August 1797, Princess Caroline adopted several foundlings and orphans from around Blackheath and placed them with local women who brought them in the daytime to her home at Montague House. '[I]t is my only amusement,' she said, 'and [they are] the only little creature[s] to which I can really attach myself.' She frankly admitted her loneliness, saying that she adopted the children because 'every Body must love something in this world'.[25]

None of these relations were made any easier by a return of the king's madness at various times between 1801 and 1804, and by an accusation of adultery levelled at Princess Caroline by Lady Douglas, the wife of a soldier, Sir John

Douglas, who lived near the princess in Blackheath. Rumours also flew around that the princess had been pregnant in 1802. Finally, in 1806, a Commission of Inquiry was launched to consider the allegations against her. The commission's report exonerated the princess, more or less, but offered numerous examples of her extravagantly wounded behaviour and her lack of political savvy. George III was upset at what he called Caroline's 'Levity and profligacy', and decided to cut all intimate and friendly contact with her.[26] Subsequent displays of what the king called 'outward marks of civility', which meant that he was polite to his daughter-in-law in public but would no longer see her in private, exacerbated the princess's loneliness and did not bode well for the future.[27]

During the next four years, the king's health declined, and took a final turn for the worse just before his youngest daughter, Amelia, died of consumption in November 1810 at the age of twenty-seven. In 1810, George III was seventy-two, a man plunged already into old age. He was frail and almost blind, unable to identify people by sight. At the end of October, familiar symptoms of his madness appeared. He began talking hurriedly, wildly and scatologically. Few around him had hopes of a permanent recovery, although no immediate steps were taken by Tory ministers to put forward a Regency Bill that might result in their dismissal and replacement with a Whig government.

For a while at the beginning of 1811 the doctors held out hope that the king was recovering, but as the weeks passed without any change in his condition a Regency Bill could not be delayed for long. At this point the prince disappointed most of his Whig friends by declaring to the prime minister, Spencer Perceval, his 'intention not to remove from their stations . . . his Majesty's official servants'.[28] In one sense the prince's decision to keep the incumbent Tory administration was pragmatic: it allowed for continuity if the king should recover. The Act of Parliament declaring the Regency was finally passed on 5 February 1811. The Prince of Wales was formally sworn in as Regent at Carlton House the next day, when ministers and officials lined up to kiss his hand, Prime Minister Spencer Perceval chief among them. For George, the time had finally come to govern, if not to rule.

4
Regent of Style

Under the terms of the act that enabled the Regency, George III was suspended from carrying out his royal functions and the Prince of Wales, as Regent, assumed their discharge on behalf of the king and in his name. The Prince Regent was vested with full royal powers, and was therefore king in all but name. As he had declared that he would before the passing of the Regency Act, the prince kept on the Tory administration, showing little inclination, even after it was clear that his father would not recover, to make any change in the government. To his old Whig allies, this inaction was dismaying confirmation that the prince's political priorities, shaken by the French Revolution and the long subsequent wars, had shifted away from them.

George's lack of active involvement in government lay partly in his indolence. He continued to dislike official business, grumbling that, 'Playing at King is no sinecure.'[1] But he had also lost any taste for political change. When the prime minister, Spencer Perceval, was bizarrely assassinated by a disgruntled debtor in May 1812, the prince made it clear that he wanted an all-party administration. Both men he chose as potential prime ministers, the Tory Richard Wellesley and the Whig Earl of Moira, refused to lead a government in such circumstances. By the end of the first week in June, only four weeks after Perceval's assassination, George reappointed all the ministers of the Perceval administration, with Lord Liverpool at their head. Whether this was shrewd politicking or pragmatic laziness was unclear; but the Whigs were left out and Tory rule continued.

Lord Liverpool was an experienced politician; he took the issue of Catholic emancipation off the table, and succeeded in holding the administration together through the remaining years of war and the domestic crises that followed, right up until his retirement after a stroke in 1827. From the time Lord Liverpool became prime minister, until the crisis over Catholic emancipation became acute years later when he was king, George took little detailed interest in the day-to-day activities of government. He continued to follow the progress of the long wars closely, but restricted his domestic involvement to necessary meetings and signings of papers.

In defiance of any notion that his more public role should be accompanied by a show of economy in keeping with the needs of the times, the prince started the new era of the Regency as he meant to continue. On 19 June 1811, despite the fact that his debts still amounted to over half a million pounds, he threw a grand fête at Carlton House, notionally for exiled members of the French royal family, but actually and symbolically to inaugurate his regency. Over two thousand invitations were despatched; one of the state rooms was hung with blue silk decorated with fleurs-de-lys, and the prince welcomed his French royal guests there, dressed in a newly designed uniform of a field marshal, a rank to which his father had never promoted him.

Breathless accounts of the banquet that night spoke of a fountain springing from the middle of the prince's table and goldfish swimming in specially constructed silver troughs embanked with mossy plants and flowers, but in fact the splendour was as much a matter of adaptation and embellishment as of new construction. The plan of the dinner tables in the fan-vaulted neo-Gothic conservatory drawn up for that night shows that the water feature did not sprout from the prince's table as report had it, but from a pond or fountain that probably already existed there.[2] This did not stop the poet Shelley claiming that the fête cost £120,000, and nothing could staunch more general criticism of the prince's profligacy and cavalier attitude to the public purse at a time when many were suffering poverty and hardship.

The contrast with George III, both in the present and the past, could not have been greater, and since the cause of the prince's extravagance lay partly in his father's parsimony, he was unlikely ever to change. He was never able and never really felt the need to keep within his income. George was generous as well as extravagant, as fond of giving pensions as he was parties and presents. Mrs Fitzherbert, now finally removed from his affections and supplanted by Lady Hertford, was pensioned off in 1811. George gave her £10,000 a year and he went on adding to his pension bill with other generous rewards for service. At his death, his annual pension bill stood at £20,000. Though his personal debts were paid off by his private estate, the pensions he had granted would have to be defrayed by the taxpayer.

From the time he had his own household, George was an expansive patron, an inveterate buyer and commissioner, and a builder who took a personal and genuine interest in the details of interior decoration in particular. Since he also hated to be alone, his interests centred on places, spaces, pastimes and occasions that allowed him to be in congenial company. As a young man, he had seized every opportunity for jaunts and visits: to the races, to the drawing rooms of his Whig friends, to clubs and dinners, to the play and the opera, bare-knuckle fights and boxing matches. He watched the first manned balloon flight in England take off from the Royal Artillery Ground on the edge of the City of London in September 1784, Signor Lunardi aboard, accompanied by a dog, a cat and a pigeon in a cage. He often attended lectures at the Royal Institution and especially enjoyed the annual dinners at the Royal Academy.

Children who came to visit the prince found stacks of toys that he had bought for them to play with, and he was always happy to join in their fun or, later, if he was at Windsor, take them in his phaeton to the menagerie in the park, a private zoo stocked with exotic creatures and birds. He could write tenderly to children he was fond of, and often gave them presents to take away.

The prince's favourite pastime was always music. He liked nothing better than an evening at the piano, when he would sing opera favourites and popular songs in his light and pleasant tenor voice. He also showed admiration for musicians, a quality that demanded humility in himself. When Gioachino Rossini visited London and Buckingham Palace in 1823, George accompanied him on the piano while he sang, and apologized for failing to keep good time. Rossini was suitably impressed, telling his host that '[t]here are few in your Royal

Highness's position who could play so well', and then swiftly asked for 'God Save the King' to be played.[3]

Literature was a less sociable pastime than music, although shortly after he became king, George agreed to sponsor a new Royal Society of Literature to 'reward literary merit and patronage; to excite literary talent by premiums', as the *Literary Gazette* put it in its announcement of the society's foundation.[4] Yet here too the prince showed skill, especially if he wasn't penning his interminable love letters. He had a polished writing style, and could turn an elegant phrase when he wished to. When the Duke of Wellington – a man he admired and disliked in equal measure – sent a letter resigning as commander-in-chief of the army in 1827, George replied with cutting brevity: 'The King assures the Duke of Wellington that the King receives the Duke's resignation of the offices of Commander-in-Chief and Master-General of the Ordnance with the same sentiments of deep regret with which the Duke states himself to offer it. The King abstains from any further expression of his feelings.'[5]

The depth of George's private reading as an adult is uncertain, but he was certainly well educated and an efficient skimmer, and in his last years was reported to have read a good deal. He remembered his reading well enough to engage Lord Byron in half an hour's conversation about poets and poetry in 1812.[6] He declared that he had read deeply in French literature of the seventeenth century, citing Madame de Sévigné, Madame de La Fayette and Madame de Bavière, whom his sceptical listener Dorothea Lieven did not try to identify, but who was almost certainly the Princess Palatine, Elizabeth Charlotte of Bavaria.[7] He became obsessed with Napoleon, and bought every book he could find about him, adding them to his library in Carlton House. Through his librarian, James Stanier Clarke, he made it known to Jane Austen, when she visited the library in 1815, that she might, if she wished, dedicate her novel *Emma*, to him, though it was, as Clarke put it, 'certainly not *incumbent* on you' to do so.[8] She did.

Though he certainly read and enjoyed Jane Austen, Walter Scott was George's favourite among living writers. Scott was the most popular author in Europe in the first half of the nineteenth century, and largely responsible for the cult of Romantic Scotland that caught up not only a huge reading audience, but the theatre, opera and music, as well as any Scots themselves. A self-consciously archaizing creation of tradition was Scott's hallmark, and it appealed to the prince just as much as the plundering of global styles that went on in his creation of the Pavilion at Brighton. He could quote extensively from Scott's works, and recite reams of *The Lay of the Last Minstrel*, and other poems.

It was perhaps in this archaizing spirit that George encouraged the publication of the surviving papers of the Stuart kings and a biography of James II. In 1823, moreover, he gave his father's entire collection of books, maps and pamphlets to the British Museum, which had been founded in 1753. The donation of the King's Library prompted the demolition of the existing museum and its replacement with a new building that would house both library and museum.

In the creation of a public gallery for the enjoyment of painting and sculpture, however, the British royal family lagged behind other European monarchs and governments. The Habsburgs had opened the Vienna Picture Gallery in

the Belvedere Palace in 1781 and the Louvre had been trans-
formed into a public museum in 1791. The National Gallery
was finally established in 1824, though not with a starting
point in the Royal Collection, as so many European national
galleries had either by design or when monarchies were
downgraded or abolished.[9]

If the prince was nothing like the great collector of books
that his father had been, he made up for it in the enthusiastic
acquisition, and often design, of robes, clothes and ceremonial garb of all kinds. As a young man setting out to oppose
the simple habits of his father, he cultivated a fastidious and
knowledgeable appreciation of cloth, fashion and fine dress.
He demanded the highest standards of his tailors. Button
placings, fabrics, linings and trimmings: all had frequently
to be replaced or altered. Repeated alterations meant that
one particular coat cost £600.

In his youth, the prince was a leader of fashion and style.
He insisted that envelopes addressed to him be folded in
a particular, and complicated, 'French fashion'.[10] He took
similar care with his clothes. For his first address to Parliament, he wore a black velvet suit, embroidered with gold
thread and lined in pink satin, with pink heels to his shoes
and his hair frizzed and curled. He ordered not just quality
but also quantity. By the time of the Regency, he owned
hundreds of dress suits and, between 1811 and 1820, bought
at least five hundred shirts. He was very fond of military
uniforms, both to design and wear and to collect. When he
wanted distraction in 1829 from duties that distressed him,
he amused himself 'devising a new dress for the Guards', and

he had eight field marshals' full-dress uniforms in his wardrobe by the time he died.[11]

After the age of thirty-five, much of George's tailoring was carefully crafted to hide his enormous bulk, about which he was extremely sensitive. His morning gowns were cut extra-wide and very long, and he usually wore 'a huge white neckcloth of many folds, out of which his chin seemed to be always struggling to emerge', as one visitor put it.[12] For a long time he resisted the fashion for trousers, which had the triple disadvantage of having been taken up in post-Revolutionary France, of being introduced into Britain by his erstwhile friend Beau Brummel, and of being best suited to the dandy elegance and slim form that Brummel made fashionable. But he wore them in the end, covered with a long jacket or coat. Although he clung to the embroidery and bright colours of his youth, he also gradually adopted even the buff, chestnut, dark blue and black of Brummell's outfits, and kept gaudy attire for ceremonial and theatrical moments, such as official levees or his trip to Scotland in 1822.

Dress and all its associated pleasures of jewels and trinkets allowed the prince to indulge his compulsive need not just to spend, but collect and keep. Like many people who have lacked consistent affection in childhood, George seems to have found it impossible to throw anything away. He acquired the habit of accumulation early and it never left him. A huge quantity of stuff was cleared out and auctioned off after his death, and we will never know the scope and size of this strange collection, or what it might have told us about the man who made it. Writing in her self-conscious and priggish diary after the king's death in 1830, the Duke of Wellington's friend Mrs Arbuthnot recorded the duke's horror at finding 'trinkets of all sorts, quantities of women's gloves, dirty snuffy pocket handkerchiefs with old faded nosegays tied up in them'. The fastidious Wellington was disgusted. '[S]uch a collection of trash he had never seen before,' he declared, and 'said he thought the best thing w^d be to burn them all.'[13] This is what seems to have happened; no trace of this stuff is left in the Royal Collection.

One record survives of what the less public spaces of the prince's residences might have contained. A whole attic storey of Carlton House, three large apartments run together, contained the prince's 'Armory'. This huge collection of weaponry and other military dress and objects from all over the world was arranged for display, if not freely available for visits. Some of it was imperial spoil, including the 'chair of state, the footstool, and sceptre of the King of Candy' and a 'suit of horse-armour and costume belong[ing] to the late Tippoo Saib'. Elsewhere there were 'caps, turbans, shields, bows, arrows, and other missiles of the Eastern nations; bows, arrows, spears, shields, battle-axes and other implements military and domestic, also various dresses, of the inhabitants of the southern hemisphere' and spurs and boots worn by particular generals. Some things, such as the 'dagger of Gengis Khan', had, in the definiteness of their attribution, a strong hint of fakery about them.[14]

While he waited to inherit the throne, George amassed his vast collections without the space to put much on display. Eventually, as king, he moved much of his art collection to the new state rooms of the enlarged Buckingham Palace and the series of state rooms and the grand corridor at Windsor Castle, the design, construction and hanging of which he oversaw very closely. Other pieces and collections were sent to various royal residences; many of the things he wanted to see and enjoy for himself went to the Brighton Pavilion and his private rooms at Windsor.

As history painting declined at the end of the eighteenth century, fineness of execution took over from the idea of fineness of representation as a way of judging and valuing a painting. In upholding this new standard, which extolled exquisite brushwork and accuracy of depiction, the prince was typical of his time. The representation of grand ideas or historical events held no attraction for him. He bought no history painting at all and almost completely eschewed the mid to late eighteenth-century taste in mythic and neo-classical fable, landscape and figuration. Of the British artists who championed history painting, he was interested only in Sir Joshua Reynolds, buying several of Reynolds's paintings after the artist's death.

In common with other collectors of his time and in keeping with this new standard, George focused on genre painting and landscape, with a particular emphasis on seventeenth-century paintings from the Low Countries: the Dutch Golden Age. His collection of Dutch painting, the core of which was acquired from Sir Thomas Baring in 1814, and first hung in Carlton House and then divided between Buckingham Palace and Windsor, was of the highest standard. The prized qualities of freshness of touch, skill in handling paint and in depicting light, shade and detail were everywhere on display. By 1819 over seventy-five Dutch and Flemish paintings hung in Carlton House, displayed in groups.

Not surprisingly, Rembrandt reigned supreme over the whole collection. The prince bought three Rembrandts to add to the two his father had acquired, handing over the staggering sum of 5,000 guineas in 1811 for the large double portrait *The Ship Builder and his Wife* of 1633. He eventually hung a very fine Rembrandt self-portrait of 1642 in his dressing room at Windsor Castle, where he must have looked at it every day during his lengthy toilette.

Alongside Rembrandt, the prince collected landscapes, sea-scapes, streetscapes and interiors, and was particularly fond of scenes of merrymaking and enjoyment – music-playing, tavern-singing, skating – with multiple figures complemented by dogs, musical instruments, wine glasses and song sheets. He placed works such as Jan Steen's *Merrymakers in a Tavern*, painted about 1670, with contemporary versions of the same sort of scene: David Wilkie's *Blind Man's Buff* of 1812–13 and Edward Bird's *Village Choristers* of 1810, which the prince bought that year for 250 guineas, on the advice of the President of the Royal Academy, Benjamin West. *Village Choristers* was a homely version of the way the prince liked to think of himself: full of good cheer and conviviality. It depicted his favourite pastime, music-making with congenial companions. George's purchases, then, reflect not just prevailing taste, but his own habits. Although he commissioned large numbers of portraits of relatives and other dignitaries, his heart remained with genre paintings such as these.

The prince took great comfort from things, and lots of them. This need, accompanied by a good eye and some overall, if wayward, aesthetic vision, was what governed his interior decoration schemes, especially that of the Royal Pavilion in Brighton. At Windsor Castle and Buckingham Palace, the prince was constrained by the public nature of the buildings and the uses to which they would be put. It was in Brighton that he could let his imagination run riot, and the Pavilion, with its eclectic mishmash of objects, colours and styles, turned out to have a life of its own. Of all surviving royal interiors, the hectic rooms of the Brighton Pavilion best transmit the personality of their creator. This, rather than the chestnut, cream, black and dark blue of Beau Brummel's sartorial palette, is the prince's design legacy. Regency style, as we tend to think of it, is Beau Brummell style. The real Regency style, the Prince Regent style, was bright and contrastingly coloured, sparkling, feverish and anything but restrained.

Had the prince been able to travel to the continent before he inherited the throne, he would surely have been an enthusiastic consumer of Europe's congenial spa culture, with its bathing, medicinal quaffing of mineral waters, music, walks and sociability. Forced to remain in Britain, he never bought a country estate, but instead made Brighton into his own spa, at least until his sensitivity about his bulk meant that he stopped sea-bathing in 1806. The Pavilion was his Xanadu, his stately pleasure dome.

In 1815, before the last round of alterations to its exterior started, the Pavilion was in an unfinished state, and plain in appearance. Francophile style, both inside and out, had dominated its first incarnation, but now the prince asked the architect John Nash to expand and redesign the whole building. It is not clear where the prince and Nash

1. Detail from a portrait of Queen Charlotte with her children, by Benjamin West, 1779. George stands on the left, manly and plump at seventeen, with his brother Frederick leaning on his shoulder.

2. The Prince of Wales in a painting by George Stubbs, 1791. The gentleman of fashion in the blue and buff of the Whigs, riding in Hyde Park at the age of twenty-nine.

3 and 4. Companion
miniatures of Prince
George and Mrs
Fitzherbert just before
their first rupture, by
Richard Cosway,
1793 and 1789.

5. Carlton House in a coloured engraving by T. Rowlandson and A. C. Pugin, 1809. The house was demolished in 1824. Later, some of its columns were reused on the front of the National Gallery.

6. *Presenting the Trophies*, Rowlandson's cheery dig at the Prince Regent's love of military memorabilia. The print shows the interior of Carlton House and Captain Johnny Newsome presenting George with Marshal Jourdan's baton and Joseph Bonaparte's hat in 1815.

7. The Peterloo Massacre in a coloured engraving published by Richard Carlile, showing the violent military response to the gathering at St Peter's Field, Manchester, on 16 August 1819.

8. George Cruikshank's engraving of the Cato Street conspirators being arrested, published March 1820. The foiling of the conspirators' plot to assassinate Cabinet ministers was a put-up job by a police informer.

9. George IV was a talented designer and inveterate wearer of military uniforms, despite the fact that he never served in the army or navy.

10. The sixty-year-old king looking suspiciously youthful in Sir Thomas Lawrence's portrait of 1822.

11. Detail from George Hayter's monumental *Trial of Queen Caroline*, 1820. The queen sits in a armchair, while lawyers from both sides confer in the foreground and the future prime minister, Lord Grey, holds forth from the floor.

12. The Prince of Wales's eye from a copy of the picture he sent to Maria Fitzherbert in 1785: a spooky reminder of his devotion.

13. Another watcher, this time looking at the prince: Rembrandt, in a self-portrait of 1642. George hung this picture in his dressing room.

14. *An Evening Landscape with Figures and Sheep* by Aelbert Cuyp, 1655–9. This exquisitely tranquil scene was in the collection of Sir Thomas Baring before being bought by the Prince Regent in 1814.

15. The exterior of the Royal Pavilion at Brighton, from John Nash's *Views of the Royal Pavilion*, 1826. A fantasy in neo-Mughal style, the Pavilion was likened by one critical visitor to the Kremlin in Moscow.

16. The Chinese Gallery in another illustration from Nash's *Views*. In contrast to the blinding white exterior, the interior was a riot of colour, with stained glass, statues and giant chandeliers.

17. George IV in Highland dress, by David Wilkie, 1830.
The costume was made for the king's Scottish visit at a cost of £1,354
18s. In 2005 the jacket was discovered by experts from Sotheby's at
Schloss Marienburg, a castle still owned by the royal house of Hanover.

got all their ideas for the 'neo-Mughal' exterior that was begun in 1815, though a wholesale borrowing or appropriation and reinvention of global cultural styles had been going on in Britain for some time. By 1762, the gardens at Kew were adorned with a pagoda, an 'Alhambra' and a 'Mosque', while Sezincote House in Gloucestershire, which the prince visited in 1810, offered a full-scale example of neo-Mughal style. Chinoiserie and Chinese or 'India' wallpaper had long been a feature of fashionable interiors, including, after 1801, that of the Pavilion itself.

The new Pavilion, which was finally finished in 1822, kept to the neo-Mughal style on the outside. This was extraordinary enough, but on the inside, where the prince really lavished his attention, there was no pre-existing dominant aesthetic. The riotous melange of styles, glorious or horrendous according to taste, was the prince's own. He hired the father and son decorating firm of John and Frederick Crace and the artist Robert Jones to design and execute the whole scheme, but frequently intervened himself if the results were not to his liking. An entry of 1820 in the Craces' account book about the walls of the Music Room records the decorators '[r]epainting the [imitation] ribbons Lilac, instead of blue, by order of His Majesty'.[15] Five years earlier, on 15 August 1815, the Craces recorded '[a]ttending His Royal Highness with 9 assistants putting in patterns to Small Drawing Room, arranging the pictures, India paper &c in Yellow Drawing Room; putting in patterns to Entrance Hall and Gallery and arranging Mr Jone[s]'s pictures', one of many such entries in their accounts.[16]

Once inside the finished Pavilion, visitors were amazed,

impressed and often stupefied. It seemed to many to be an enchanted palace, with colours shifting through stained glass, and light glancing and twinkling from lanterns, mirrors, chandeliers and lacquered walls. Glittering objects filled the rooms: gilt conch-shells, silvered dragons and snakes, and gilded furniture. Everything was saturated with colour – deep reds, yellows, blues. Carpets throbbed with brightness and pattern. Perfumes suffused the air; the rooms were warmed by underfloor heating and hung with heavy silk curtains. The kitchens were ornamented with columns of cast iron in the shape of palm trees and hexagonal lanterns.

Those who loved colour, fantasy and extravagance were carried away by the eccentric brilliance of the Pavilion. Others resisted its charm. The diarist John Wilson Croker, who visited in 1818, declared that the exterior 'is said to be taken from the Kremlin at Moscow', while the loquacious Princess Lieven was lost for words. 'How can one describe such a piece of architecture [as] the King's palace here?' she wrote to Prince Metternich, in stunned amazement. 'The style is a mixture of Moorish, Tartar, Gothic and Chinese, and all in stone and iron.' Everyone speculated about the costs. 'We were shown a chandelier which cost eleven thousand pounds sterling,' the princess wrote, and added that the whole building had cost £700,000, while Charles Greville reported that the subterranean passage from the Pavilion to the stables had cost £3,000, if not £5,000.[17]

Like the decor, the food at the Pavilion was extravagant, and could be superb. Antonin Carême, the famous French chef, ran the kitchens for eight months in 1816–17, offering the choicest of modern French dishes. Still, the parties could be dull; after his first visit in 1821, Greville wrote that he never wanted to go again and 'be exposed to the whole weight of the bore of it without the stimulus of curiosity', though he did, in fact, return the next year.[18]

Life in Brighton became more staid as George grew older and more infirm. He sometimes trotted about on the lawns of the Pavilion, having been pulled up an inclined ramp in his chair, and then lowered on to his horse. Much of the time he spent indoors with his mistress Lady Hertford – and after her with his last mistress Lady Conyngham, whom he got to know in 1819, and who took over the arduous post of royal companion in 1820. The turbulence of his marital life briefly seemed to be receding; the Princess of Wales's wish to live abroad had been growing stronger since the beginning of the Regency, and in the summer of 1814 she finally left. A year later, the nineteen-year-old Princess Charlotte, who had rebelled against her father's authority, and refused to marry his choice of Prince William of Orange, was happily engaged to Prince Leopold of Saxe-Coburg-Saalfeld, a solemn, intelligent and impecunious adventurer, who had rented rooms above a grocer's in Marylebone High Street from which to press his suit.

The marriage of Princess Charlotte and Prince Leopold took place in May 1816, and by the following year they were expecting a child and living contentedly in Clermont Park in Surrey. On 5 November 1817, after fifty hours of labour, the princess delivered a stillborn boy. A few hours later she died herself, leaving the Prince Regent without an heir, and his younger brothers Frederick and William suddenly in line for the throne. Although the prince had never been close to his

75

daughter, whom he regarded as too like her mother to be endearing, he was horrified by her death, and still unable to read out a speech containing her name the following summer.

The Duke of Wellington had disliked Princess Charlotte, and called her death 'a blessing to the country'. The lawyer and MP Henry Brougham, however, declared that it 'produced throughout the Kingdom feelings of the deepest sorrow and most bitter disappointment'.[19] Prince Leopold was devastated; he did not believe in the Regent's grief, and lived on in bitter retirement at Clermont Park until his surprising elevation as King of the Belgians in 1831.

Not a single one of George's surviving siblings had so far produced a legitimate child and an heir to the throne in the next generation was desperately needed. George's unmarried brothers needed to step forward, and, summarily abandoning existing ties, they did. Both William, Duke of Clarence, who had lived for years with the actress Mrs Jordan, and Edward, Duke of Kent, who had a long-term liaison with a Madame Saint-Laurent, managed to get married in 1818. The Duke and Duchess of Clarence's two baby daughters died shortly after birth. The Duke and Duchess of Kent were luckier. Their daughter, Princess Victoria, was born in 1819. She was, and remained, the only legitimate grandchild of George III's huge family of sons and daughters who lived long enough to become the sovereign.

The prince had assumed the Regency at a time when the war with France showed no signs of dying down or coming to a close. The tide finally turned in 1812, when Napoleon's disastrous invasion of Russia signalled the beginning of the end for the First French Empire. After the long retreat from Moscow, Napoleon was defeated in mid October 1813 at the Battle of the Nations near Leipzig in Saxony by a combined allied force of Russia, Prussia, Austria and Sweden. In 1814 the allies invaded France both from the north and from Spain. On 31 March, the allied powers occupied Paris. Napoleon abdicated on 6 April, and it seemed that the long wars were over.

In Britain, the Prince Regent welcomed Louis XVI's brother, the Count of Provence, now Louis XVIII (the dauphin, technically Louis XVII, having died at the age of ten in 1795) to London, from his place of exile in Buckinghamshire. A few days later, he accompanied the new king to Dover and waved him off for France from the end of the pier. With one sovereign gone, George prepared to welcome others. The victorious monarchs were gathering in Britain to celebrate their victory. Frederick William III, King of Prussia, Tsar Alexander I and Prince Metternich, as the representative of the Emperor of Austria, arrived on 7 June. Alexander was accompanied by the Cossack commander, Count Platov, Frederick William by his commander, Field Marshal Blücher. The tsar's sister, the Grand Duchess of Oldenburg, completed the royal party.

Celebrations and junkets did little to disguise the dislike George and the tsar soon developed for one another. The bluff King of Prussia annoyed the Prince Regent not with his elegance, vanity or superior experience on the battlefield, as the tsar did, but by his rejection of the state bed that had been made and put up for him at Clarence House in favour of a camp bed on the floor. The whole visit none the less passed off satisfactorily, though the peace and victory that the sovereigns' visit was to celebrate were nullified the next year by Napoleon's escape from Elba on 26 February 1815 and by the need to mobilize the allied armies all over again.

The Prince Regent received the news of final victory at Waterloo while he was at a party in St James's Square at the house of a Mrs Boehm. A commotion outside alerted the guests to the arrival of a dusty, exhausted Major Percy, who ran up the steps to the house with two French regimental flags, and laid them at the Regent's feet with the words, 'Victory, sir! victory!' The party instantly broke up, and George took himself off to a side room to read the despatches, emerging a while later into the nearly empty ballroom. 'It is a glorious victory, and we must rejoice at it, but the loss of life has been fearful, and I have lost many friends,' he said, and tears ran down his cheeks.[20]

In Britain, the maintenance of the Tory government under the long administration of Lord Liverpool had stabilized the day-to-day domestic political environment. Until the final defeat of Napoleon, the forces that threatened domestic stability were kept in check, though increasing poverty led to rioting and machine breaking in industrial areas in the last years of the war. Huge amounts of wealth were being transferred to Britain from imperial possessions. On the Indian subcontinent, the East India Company had continued its conquests unabated with expansion into Nepal and the Punjab. In Africa, the Cape Colony, annexed in 1806, formally became a British possession in 1814. Elsewhere during the long wars, Britain acquired Trinidad,

Tobago, St Lucia, Mauritius, British Guiana and Ceylon (now Guyana and Sri Lanka).

Despite this wealth, political and social unrest grew inexorably in Britain. After 1815, a series of poor harvests, together with continued industrialization and high unemployment, not least among returning soldiers, added to domestic turmoil. Discontent and poverty combined to force into the open the great political issues of the day: the reform of Parliament and the franchise, and Catholic emancipation. On 16 August 1819, after a series of huge meetings around the country, an immense crowd of more than sixty thousand people gathered on St Peter's Field in Manchester to call for universal suffrage and annual parliaments. Order appeared to be threatened. As tension mounted, the Manchester Yeomanry and the 15th Regiment of Hussars attacked the crowd. Fifteen people were killed and hundreds wounded in the melee, which was immediately called the Peterloo Massacre. As its name suggested, the era of the European convulsions that culminated in Waterloo was over. The stage was set for the next century of politics, which would be dominated by the empire and by domestic concerns, particularly the need to widen the franchise.

The Liverpool government was well aware of the potential for massive unrest after Peterloo. Parliament was recalled to debate the issue. The Prince Regent, who had been sensitive to any perceived threat to the monarchy ever since the French Revolution, declared in his opening speech that 'the seditious practices so long prevalent in some of the manufacturing districts of the country have . . . led to proceedings incompatible with the public tranquillity, and with the peaceful habits of the industrious classes of the community; and a spirit is now fully manifested, utterly hostile to the constitution of this kingdom.'[21]

Parliament passed a series of acts in December 1819 to curb outdoor gatherings and limit seditious publications, and the threat of more violence was averted. Although, in February 1820, several men from a revolutionary organization, which had already been involved in riots in Spa Fields on the edge of the City of London a few years earlier, were arrested and charged with plotting to assassinate the Cabinet and provoke a revolution, the tide had turned against violent agitation. Infiltrated and set up by a police spy, the Cato Street conspirators, as they were called, were found guilty, and their five leaders hanged. Republican sentiment and revolutionary zeal were thereafter dissipated.

In the cultural sphere, too, literary and philosophical radicalism was on the wane. It had been declining since the death of the publisher Joseph Johnson in 1809 and the dissolution of his circle by death, old age and emigration. Mary Wollstonecraft, Johnson's friend and protégée, had died in 1797; her husband William Godwin turned to writing and publishing children's books soon after the turn of the century, in an effort to shore up his finances. Joseph Priestley had died in 1804 in Pennsylvania. Lord Byron, whose maiden speech in the House of Lords in 1812 championed destitute weavers, was drummed out of the country in 1816. He died in 1824, still in exile and fighting for Greek independence. His fellow poet Percy Bysshe Shelley wrote *The Mask of Anarchy*, his famous 1819 exhortation to the 'Men of England' to rise up after the Peterloo Massacre ('Ye are many – they are few'), also in exile, on the Tuscan coast. He himself died in 1822. William Wordsworth had gone into rural reaction in the Lake District. Samuel Taylor Coleridge was lowered by depression and addiction. The presiding genius of the times was Prince George's favourite, Sir Walter Scott, for whom 1819 was a peak year for sales. This cultural shift was, as so often, in advance of wider change. Peterloo signalled to those in power that they would have to use the powers of Parliament, both carrot and stick, to take the heat out of radical demands; the wider shift in sentiment meant that reform could be delayed for some time, and, when it came, could be offered piecemeal.

5
King at Last

The Tory politician George Canning, who later said that 'there was not a man of property who did not tremble for his possessions', felt confident enough to declare in March 1820 that November 1819 and January 1820 effectively belonged to two different epochs in the nation's history. By the end of January, Canning declared, political stability, property rights, 'domestic tranquillity' and the 'moral and religious sense' of the nation had been restored.[1] If some men of property breathed sighs of relief, many others had barely registered the threat to their peace and prosperity. Indeed, for many, good times seemed never to have gone away. Charles Greville, man about town, gossip merchant and clerk to the Privy Council, used his diary not only to record day-to-day events but also to capture the tone of ruling-class life. In 1818, when he was twenty-four, the days seemed indolent and good; he and his fellow guests at a house party were 'trifl[ing] life away'. In 1819 Peterloo came and went, barely disturbing him.

At the end of January 1820, Greville was again in luxurious surroundings, at Woburn House, where he 'shot the whole week and killed an immense quantity of game; the last two days we killed 245 and 296 pheasants'.[2] Important news did not stop the carnage. 'On Sunday last arrived the news of the King's death,' Greville wrote simply, before adding: 'The new King has been desperately ill. He had a bad cold at Brighton, for which he lost eighty ounces of blood; yet he afterwards had a severe oppression, amounting almost to suffocation, on his chest.'[3]

So an aged and incapacitated king was replaced by an ailing one. George III was eighty-one when he died at Windsor on 29 January 1820, George IV fifty-seven when he finally inherited the throne. After a lifetime of waiting, he initially had no strength to carry out his duties. Too weak to attend his father's funeral, he spent the days before it ill and preoccupied with the question of his marriage. His hated wife Caroline was now the queen, and she had every right to return to Britain. The opposition wanted her at least to come closer, to put pressure on the government. Very soon the matter had become urgent because, somewhat to the dismay of her lawyer, the MP Henry Brougham, Caroline was back. Without official recognition, she took an ordinary passenger boat from Calais, and landed at Dover on 5 June 1820.

At once Caroline became the focus of intense emotion. 'The discussion of the Queen's business is now become an intolerable nuisance in society,' Greville wrote in his diary. 'It is an incessant matter of argument and dispute what will be done and what ought to be done. All people express themselves tired of the subject, yet none talk or think of any other.'[4] The problem was not just George IV's implacable hatred of the queen; it was that Caroline became almost overnight the channel for public anger about issues that had nothing to do with her. She immediately became the symbol of monarchical high-handedness, political intransigence and a general feeling that the government and the king were as indifferent towards the rights and needs of ordinary people as they were to the rights of the queen. A disgruntled public flocked to her cause.

Parliamentarians of all persuasions were rattled. Lord Grey, the Whig leader, future prime minister and architect of the Reform Act of 1832, declared that if something was not done to address political concerns, Britain would see 'a Jacobin Revolution more bloody than that of France'.[5] The king, however, was unequivocal. He wanted Caroline to be forbidden the title of queen, and he wanted to divorce her on the grounds of alleged adultery with her Italian companion Bartolomeo Pergami. George's agents had tracked the queen around Europe and taken testimony from a host of witnesses about numerous incidents in inns, in villas and in the cabin of a boat on which Caroline had sailed to the Holy Land. Now the king was determined to bring his wife to trial.

The queen's trial – technically the reading of (i.e. debate on) a Bill of Pains and Penalties brought before the House of Lords on 5 July 1820 – was both highly sensational and severely compromised by the large sums of money paid to witnesses on both sides. Henry Brougham believed his client guilty and increasingly disliked her; yet he was bound to her defence by both principle and expediency. Caroline drew strength from the king's unpopularity. Crowds accompanied her carriage to the House every day; demonstrations filled the streets of London. Notwithstanding the weight of the evidence, many believed that the case against the queen was concocted and the witnesses merely bought for cash. When the Lords eventually voted on the bill, the majority in its favour was so small that the government knew it could never pass the House of Commons, particularly since Brougham had shrewdly got hold of a copy of George IV's will, in which he referred to Mrs Fitzherbert as his 'dear wife', thus compromising his right to the throne and to any moral high ground he might have been trying to take. So in November 1820 the bill was abandoned, although the government managed quietly to sneak through clauses that meant that Caroline would not be crowned and could not live in any royal residence.

These clauses set up the story for its sad denouement. Riotous joy greeted the abandonment of the bill. Ships in the Thames were decorated with trophies, the Duke of Wellington, who was now serving as Master-General of the Ordnance in Liverpool's administration and was seen as the figurehead of the Tory government, was loudly booed in the streets, and the foreign secretary, Lord Castlereagh, was 'roughly handled at Covent Garden'.[6] But popular fervour was dissipating. Caroline was forbidden from attending the coronation, which went ahead without her on 19 July 1821. She set out for the ceremony in her coach, but was turned away near Westminster Hall, and had to drive back to her house. Very soon afterwards she became ill; on 7 August she died.

Queen Caroline lived out, in her own particular way, the terrible hand dealt to royal princesses, who were married off and sent away, or brought in, as pawns in grand diplomatic games. Without power or choice, they were unable to have a fulfilling personal life of any kind if they were neglected by their spouses or did not love them. They were furthermore forced into complete passivity at a time when even aristocratic women had some choice over whom they married. Caroline's unfitness for this unpalatable role was obvious from the beginning. Warnings, both of the price of rebellion and the price of compliance, were all around her. Her aunt, Caroline Matilda, had been callously married at fifteen to the King of Denmark, whom British diplomats knew already to have been suffering from a complex psychosexual disorder. She rebelled, and her defiant attempt to find love and meaning in her life ended in exile and early death. Obedience was little better. Queen Charlotte, Caroline's mother-in-law, acted out her loneliness and powerlessness by isolating and terrorizing her six daughters and trying to forbid them marrying and having lives of their own. Caroline herself lived her mother's role, sidelined by a husband who was able to pursue a romantic life with a series of other women. Being a royal prince was for the most part to live a useless life; being a royal princess more likely an unhappy and powerless one.

On the day Queen Caroline died, the king arrived at Holyhead in his yacht the *Royal George*, 'in the best health and spirits'.[7] He was on his way to Ireland, taking belated advantage of his freedom to travel wherever he wished. A few days after this, the queen's coffin arrived in Harwich, where a great crowd watched it being lowered into the hold of a ship to be taken to Brunswick.

With the removal of the queen's corpse from Britain, her

haunting of the king was over. On his fifty-ninth birthday, George crossed the Irish Sea in a steamboat, carousing all the way and arriving at Howth in a very merry state. He was the first king to come to Ireland since James II and William III had fought for the English throne on Irish soil in 1690, a fact that it would have been impolitic to mention. Ireland, subdued after the failure of the Irish Rebellion of 1798, the abolition of its parliament, and the union with Great Britain, was once again in a state of turmoil. Demands for independence would soon boil up if palliative measures for Catholics were not taken. In 1811 the brilliant lawyer Daniel O'Connell had founded the Catholic Board to campaign for emancipation.

George IV may have thought that his visit would calm the country's social unease and political grievance; but he saw little of Ireland outside Dublin and the grandest houses, cosseted by the Protestant political class and by the enthusiasm of those who did turn out to see him. His Irish subjects appeared to be loyal everywhere he went, and he himself declared that his heart had always been Irish and that he loved the country. After a round of ritual and ceremony in Dublin, he left for Slane Castle in County Meath, where his mistress Lady Conyngham was waiting for him with her complaisant husband by her side, any embarrassment on his part tempered by his promotion to the British peerage and the Privy Council, as well as to the offices of Lord Steward of the Household and Constable and Governor of Windsor Castle.

When George left Ireland, after a visit of just over three weeks, it appeared to his entourage that differences between

Catholics and Protestants had been smoothed over. Daniel O'Connell presented the king with a laurel crown before he got on the boat. Yet the victory was not the king's. Two years later, O'Connell would found the Catholic Association to press not just for emancipation, which would have allowed Catholics to hold public office, but for the franchise, which would allow them, or some of them, to vote.

Only a few weeks after he arrived back from Ireland, George set off on his travels again, this time to the kingdom of Hanover, to which he had also acceded on his father's death. On the way, he stopped in Brussels, where the Duke of Wellington was waiting to receive him. A grand banquet was given for him by the King and Queen of the Netherlands at their palace at Laeken, an event that he enjoyed immensely, entertaining his hosts with a cruel and accurate imitation of a member of their family and being generally 'very blackguard and entertaining', as the Duke of Wellington put it.[8]

After a short stay in Brussels, the king visited the site of the Battle of Waterloo. The Duke of Wellington conducted the party over the battlefield, explaining the course of the battle as rain poured down. The king 'took it all very coolly', Wellington reported, and rummaged about hoping to unearth some bones. He didn't ask any questions, or even say a word, Wellington went on, 'till I showed him where Lord Anglesey's leg was buried, and then he burst into tears'.[9]

From Waterloo the party proceeded to Hanover. George entered the town on horseback, and proceeded to a hasty coronation, which was followed by parties, royal levees, when he received guests, and other junkets that exhausted him. Revived by a few days of rest, he went to the university town of Göttingen, where a fulsome address by the town's devoted citizens reduced him once more to tears.

These trips, accompanied as they were by gratifying cheers from his loyal subjects, and grand receptions, had given the king a taste for travel. The next year he was off again, this time to Scotland, travelling north by sea and landing at Leith on 15 August 1822. He had chosen his friend Sir Walter Scott to plan the outlines of the trip and be the master of ceremonies, while he himself concentrated on acquiring suitably grandiose costumes. His outfits for the whole tour cost well over a thousand pounds, made from fabric that included sixty-one yards of satin, thirty-one yards of velvet and seventeen and a half yards of cashmere, each woven in a different tartan pattern.

Scott did not disappoint him. The king was delighted with the tartan vision of Scotland that Scott served up, from a command performance of a dramatized version of his recent novel *Rob Roy*, published in 1817, to a procession through the streets of Edinburgh and a Caledonian ball where any guests who were competent accompanied paid dancers in Scottish reels.[10] When he got back to London, George summoned the Scottish painter David Wilkie to paint him in Highland dress. The king looked astonishingly sylph-like and young in the finished picture, on which Wilkie laboured until 1829.

In fact, George was prematurely aged, his body breaking apart after decades of overindulgence and lack of activity. Released from its corsets, the king's stomach now hung to his knees. After 1820 his face was usually covered in make-up when he appeared in public and his once fine brown hair was obscured or replaced with a wig. He weighed a great deal more than the seventeen stone and eight pounds recorded in 1797, when he had stood on the weighing scales at the wine merchant's Berry Bros at the age of thirty-five, but as late as the early 1820s, he was still capable of putting away three bottles of claret at dinner.

The visit to Scotland was the last long trip the king took. Henceforward he lived most of the time at the Royal Lodge at Windsor, preferring it to the Pavilion, where he was exposed much more to the public gaze. Though he continued to take a notional interest in political and public affairs, infirmity was beginning to define his life. His eyesight was failing and he was often frail and in pain. Hugely swollen legs and feet meant he was unable to move easily. Stairs defeated him, and he was often carried up and down, and pushed about in a wheeled chair. State business had to come to him since he was rarely now in London, where he had no finished residence after the demolition of Carlton House in 1826 (its columns being reused on the front of the National Gallery) to make room for the development of Carlton House Terrace and while Buckingham Palace was being rebuilt.

George Greville visited Windsor for a session of the Privy Council in June 1827, and reported that the Royal Lodge, which the king had taken over because the castle was also undergoing very extensive renovation and remodelling, 'is a delightful place to live in, but the rooms are too low and too small for very large parties. Nothing can exceed the luxury of the internal arrangements.' The king, he wrote, 'was very well and in excellent spirits, but very weak in his knees and could not walk without difficulty'.[11] By this time, the king's love for Lady Conyngham had cooled, but he remained fond of her family and still needed her company.

As Greville noted, spending, both on upkeep of the royal buildings, and on renovations, continued unabated. Even after the demolition of Carlton House, which must have cut his expenses a little, the king was paying for the Brighton Pavilion, the *Royal George* and *Prince Regent* yachts, a house at Ascot Heath, St James's Palace, Stud Lodge, Buckingham and Kensington Palaces, Cumberland Lodge, the new Royal Mews built in 1825 in the grounds of Buckingham Palace after the old mews at Charing Cross had been demolished to make way for Trafalgar Square, the Ranger's Cottage in Bushy Park, Kew Palace and Windsor Castle and its various dependencies. His income from all sources, now efficiently managed by William Knighton, Keeper of the Privy Purse, was around £90,000 a year, but even this was never enough.

The decorative pageant of the king's Irish visit had not dampened calls for Catholic emancipation, and since Catholic emancipation was inevitably connected with a more general reform of the franchise, an ominous political storm was now gathering. It was precipitated by the illness of Lord Liverpool, who had a stroke in February 1827. Pretty soon it was obvious that he would not be able to continue as prime minister and his incapacity threw the Tory government into disarray. The three senior politicians in the party, the Duke of Wellington, the home secretary Robert

Peel and the foreign secretary George Canning, could not see eye to eye, especially on the Catholic question. The king was unable to decide on whom to call after Lord Liverpool announced that he would resign, and a period of chaos ensued.

Eventually the king asked Canning to form a government, choosing to believe, against the evidence, that Canning would not press the Catholic question. Canning tried to do what the king wanted, but Peel, Wellington and many other Tories refused to join any administration he would lead. Canning was forced to turn to the moderate Whigs for support and form a kind of cross-party administration. In April 1827, he became prime minister, only to die of pneumonia four months later, expiring in the same room at Chiswick where Charles James Fox had died twenty-one years before. With Canning's death and his own increasing infirmity, the king's influence fell away, despite the fact that the political problems that had been gathering through the years of his regency and reign were now coming to a point of crisis. He had alienated many Tories by his appointment of Canning and had never regained the trust of the Whigs after his failure to bring them into government both in 1788 and at the beginning of the Regency.

After Canning died, Lord Goderich headed a short and incompetent ministry, which collapsed after a few months. Finally, in January 1828, the Duke of Wellington became prime minister, knowing that his chief task was to produce a successful resolution to the Irish question. Ireland was at boiling point, and tensions rose when Daniel O'Connell was elected MP for County Clare in July 1828 with a huge majority. As a Catholic, O'Connell could not serve in Westminster without emancipation. County Clare was therefore without representation. Unrest was sure to spread, and more elections of Catholics bound to follow. The problem would soon undermine the stability of Ireland, and therefore of all of the United Kingdom.

The Duke of Wellington was a very reluctant reformer; but he was also an Irish Protestant and a Tory. He realized that for things to stay the same – for Ireland to remain under British, and Protestant, control – things would have to change. Wellington's goal was to change them as little as possible, choosing to ignore the fact that emancipation of Catholics would soon lead to the same demand by all other non-Anglicans in the polity. Moreover, as was widely recognized, Catholic emancipation in Ireland was only the beginning. It would embolden those demanding a more general reform of the franchise in the rest of the United Kingdom. The Whigs, who had long championed such reform, were waiting in the wings.

Before Wellington could even begin to contemplate any legislation, he had the unenviable task of persuading the king that reform was inevitable. George might have been sympathetic to Whig demands for reform in his youth, but he was now more than ever opposed to it. Wellington persisted; the king was extraordinarily ingenious in turning the conversation from any subject that he didn't like, and threatened to retire to Hanover when Wellington cornered him. By January 1829 he had agreed that the Cabinet should discuss the problem, only to be stiffened against change by his brother Augustus, who arrived from Germany loudly proclaiming his devotion to the Protestant cause.

The king's avoidance behaviour was by now driving Wellington and other ministers to distraction. George pretended he had fought at the Battle of Waterloo, declared that he had helped turn the tide at the Battle of Salamanca during the Peninsular War, 'when things were looking very black indeed', and vividly described how he had won the Goodwood Cup riding 'Fleur-de-Lis'.[12]

Many of his exasperated ministers were half convinced that the king was insane, especially after one Cabinet meeting on 4 March, when he sipped brandy and water throughout, talked more or less continuously for five and a half hours and then asked them to resign. They did so, and left. By the following evening, the king had recovered his senses, given in and asked Wellington to come back. 'My Dear Friend,' he wrote with his customary opening, 'As I find the country would be left without an administration, I have decided to yield my opinion to *that* which is considered by the Cabinet to be for the immediate interests of the country.' Turning the knife at the end he wrote: 'God knows what pain it cost me to write these words. G.R.'[13]

Wellington was furious, but hurried to introduce the bill. This time he had won. The duke was '[King] Arthur' now, George said, he himself merely 'Canon of Windsor'.[14] He signed the Roman Catholic Relief Act on 10 April 1829. The act took away with one hand what it gave with the other. Catholics could henceforth hold public office and sit in Parliament. Few of them, however, could now vote: the act disenfranchised the forty-shilling freeholders, modest property-holders many of whom were Catholics, by raising the property qualification to £10.

George's self-pitying description of Wellington as king and he himself a lowly functionary was histrionic but not completely inaccurate. As foreign affairs had for a century, domestic politics now turned on forces beyond the monarch's control. The king gave way on Catholic emancipation, but emancipation, and the reforms that followed it, would have happened anyway. The 'secret influence' so feared by politicians in the eighteenth century was becoming less relevant, and a constitutional monarchy increasingly entrenched.

The Tory government got its way on Catholic Relief by mobilizing all its supporters, including those who held seats for the so-called 'rotten boroughs', where there were few, if any, voters, and which were often traded for cash, since ownership of the land brought a seat in Parliament. Anti-Catholic Tories now had a reason to support a general reform of the franchise: getting rid of rotten boroughs, they argued, would increase their parliamentary power-base. Opposition to reform of the franchise was now split: the stage was set for the Great Reform Act of 1832, which would, after the death of George IV, be the first of a series of reforms of the franchise that culminated in universal male and limited female suffrage in 1918 and finally, ten years later, to votes for all men and women over the age of twenty-one.

After the passage of the Catholic Relief Act, George took to his bed for a while. He was now suffering from a raft of ailments, including gout, rheumatism, swollen arms and legs, inflammation of the bladder and a generally disturbed peace of mind, for all of which he took large quantities of laudanum. 'He leads a most extraordinary life,' Greville recorded after a visit to Windsor: 'never gets up till six in the afternoon. They come to him and open the window curtains at six or seven o'clock in the morning; he breakfasts in bed, does whatever business he can be brought to transact in bed too, he reads every newspaper quite through, dozes three or four hours, gets up in time for dinner, and goes to bed between ten and eleven. He sleeps very ill, and rings his bell forty times in the night.'[15] By May 1829, however, he had perked up temporarily, had a happy visit from Princess Victoria – 'a short, plain-looking child' – and went up to St James's Palace to hear the celebrated mezzo-soprano Maria Malibran sing for him.[16] Lady Conyngham was still in reluctant attendance at Windsor, and even though he complained about her conduct, he seemed still to need her.

A team of doctors and apothecaries was now stationed permanently in and around Windsor, where the king was installed in the newly renovated castle, although George only really trusted William Knighton, his adviser and financial controller, who had once been a doctor himself. By the spring of 1830, the king was suffering frequent attacks of breathlessness, and had to sleep sitting and propped up with pillows. These attacks, when he struggled for breath, terrified him, and he often clung to the hand of whoever was near to him. Most of the time, however, he was brave and optimistic, despite frequent pains in his bladder. Occasionally he was able to converse, and was as lively and witty as ever. When pain troubled him, he sipped laudanum, sometimes as much as two hundred and fifty drops in thirty-six hours. Knighton was a courageous man. He took responsibility for the king's health and sensibly resisted several proposed operations, which allowed George to drift towards death as comfortably as possible.

By May there was no doubt that the sixty-seven-year-old king was failing. Mrs Fitzherbert, when she heard of his illness, finally wrote him a letter expressing her sympathies, which broke the long silence between them. The king read it with evident emotion and slipped it under his pillow. He lay on a day bed that could be pushed up to the window to allow him to see across the garden. Sometimes he was still lively and even talkative. He looked forward to visits from his sisters, and was able even on 16 June to stamp four hundred official documents in lieu of signing after a 'Signature Bill' had given his stamp the legal status of a signature. But though he told Wellington in the middle of June that he was getting better, in the early hours of 26 June he woke up and seemed to know he was dying. 'My dear boy!' he said to the doctor who was with him. 'This is death!' And so it was: when another doctor, Sir Henry Halford, came into the room, the king held on to his hand without speaking, and, 'with a very few short breathings, expired'.[17]

In his will of 1796, written when he was thirty-four years old and still Prince of Wales, George stated that he wished to be buried with his miniature of Mrs Fitzherbert hanging round his neck. It seems that in his last illness he wore it under his shirt, and he asked Wellington, as his executor, to ensure that he was buried in his nightclothes, 'with whatever ornaments might be upon his person at the time of his death'. Wellington assured him that this would be done, and it was. As the king's body lay in state in Windsor Castle on 14 July, the day before his funeral, Wellington noticed a black ribbon underneath the nightshirt. Pushing aside the collar he saw a diamond locket with Mrs Fitzherbert's portrait inside.[18] George IV had kept this gesture both as the monarch and as a private man, to the last. It was heartfelt, sentimental and theatrical, the expression of his most lasting affection.

The day after the king's funeral, Charles Greville, who had spent many hours in his company, wrote laconically in his diary: '*London, July 16th.* – I returned here on the 6th of this month, and have waited these ten days to look about me and see and hear what is passing. The present King and his proceedings occupy all attention, and nobody thinks any more of the late King than if he had been dead fifty years, unless it be to abuse him and to rake up all his vices and misdeeds.'[19]

George IV left his greatest mark on the country in physical form: the remodelled castle at Windsor, the dull bulk and facade of Buckingham Palace and the exuberant individualism of the Brighton Pavilion. The most that could be said about his handling of national affairs was that he did not, in the end, impede Catholic emancipation. That reform led to others that very gradually increased political representation while keeping the basic governing structures of the country the same.

Five months after George IV's death and the accession to the throne of his brother the Duke of Clarence as William IV, the country was thrown into political turmoil when the Duke of Wellington made an uncompromising declaration against any parliamentary reform whatsoever. His government was defeated and he resigned, leading the way for Lord Grey in 1832. A new world was coming, a world of steam trains, urban life, mass culture and greater democracy. Remarkably, though, the old world of the Tory party, of Eton and empire, would endure. By maintaining continuity with his once-hated father's principles and politics, George IV played his part in ensuring that it did.

Notes

1. FATHER AND SON

1. James Greig (ed.), *The Diaries of a Duchess: Extracts from the Diaries of the First Duchess of Northumberland (1716–1776)* (London: Hodder & Stoughton, 1926), p. 48.
2. *The Times*, 16 July 1830.
3. Charles Lamb, 'Triumph of the Whale', *Examiner*, 15 March 1812.
4. Crown Prince Frederick to his father, Frederick William I of Prussia, quoted in Janice Hadlow, *The Strangest Family: The Private Lives of George III, Queen Charlotte and the Hanoverians* (London: William Collins, 2014), p. 136.
5. Ibid., p. 138.
6. Queen Charlotte to her brother Prince Charles of Mecklenburg-Strelitz, 17 October 1778, quoted in ibid., p. 224.
7. Queen Charlotte to Prince Charles of Mecklenburg-Strelitz, 6 September 1780, quoted in ibid., p. 223.
8. Greig (ed.), *Diaries of a Duchess*, p. 63.
9. George III to the Duke of Gloucester, Royal Archives, GEO/15939–40.
10. George III to Prince of Wales and Prince Frederick, 3 May 1778, in A. Aspinall (ed.), *The Correspondence of George, Prince of Wales 1770–1812*, 8 vols (London: Cassell, 1963–71), vol. 1, p. 26.
11. Charlotte Papendiek, lady-in-waiting to Queen Charlotte, quoted in Saul David, *Prince of Pleasure: The Prince of Wales and the Making of the Regency* (London: Little, Brown, 1998), p. 17.
12. Prince of Wales to Mary Hamilton, 22 August 1779, quoted in Elizabeth and Florence Anson, eds, *Mary Hamilton* (London: John Murray, 1925), pp. 83–4.
13. George III to Prince of Wales, in ibid., p. 34; Prince of Wales to James Harris, later Earl of Malmesbury, in Third Earl of Malmesbury (ed.), *Diaries and Correspondence of James Harris, First Earl of Malmesbury*, 4 vols (London: R. Bentley, 1844), vol. 2, p. 125.
14. Henry Reeve (ed.), *The Greville Memoirs: A Journal of the Reigns of King George IV and King William IV by the Late Charles C. F. Greville, Esq.*, 3 vols (London: Longmans, Green & Co., 1875), vol. 1, p. 221.
15. Earl of Ilchester (ed.), *Elizabeth, Lady Holland, to Her Son, 1821–1845* (London: John Murray, 1946), p. 77.
16. Aspinall (ed.), *Correspondence of Prince of Wales*, vol. 1, p. 76.
17. Ibid., p. 61.
18. Ibid., p. 148.

2. GROWING AND LIVING

1. Prince of Wales to Mary Robinson, quoted in Christopher Hibbert, *George IV: Prince of Wales, 1762–1811* (London: Longman, 1972), p. 18.
2. Nathaniel Wraxall, *The Historical and the Posthumous Memoirs of Sir Nathaniel William Wraxall, 1772–1784*, ed. Henry B. Wheatley, 5 vols (London: Bickers & Son, 1884), vol. 5, p. 364.
3. Prince of Wales to Dr John Turton, quoted in Hibbert, *Prince of Wales*, p. 249.
4. Lord Holland, quoted in David, *Prince of Pleasure*, p. 257.
5. George III to Prince of Wales, in Aspinall (ed.), *Correspondence of Prince of Wales*, vol. 1, p. 156.
6. Prince of Wales to Mrs Fitzherbert, in ibid., p. 201.
7. George III to Prince of Wales, in ibid., p. 231.
8. Charles James Fox in the House of Commons, 30 April 1787, in William Cobbett (ed.), *The Parliamentary History of England, from the Earliest Period to the Year 1803*, vol. 26 (London: Longman et al., 1816), cols 1067–70.
9. George III, quoted in Thomas Moore, *Memoirs of the Life of the Right Honourable Richard Brinsley Sheridan*, vol. 2 (Paris: A. and W. Galignani, 1825), p. 83.
10. Ida Macalpine and Richard Hunter, *George III and the Mad-Business* (London: Allen Lane, 1969).
11. Official medical bulletin on the king's health, quoted in Hibbert, *Prince of Wales*, p. 97.
12. Edmund Burke to Captain J. W. Payne, 24 September 1789, in Aspinall (ed.), *Correspondence of Prince of Wales*, vol. 2, p. 35.
13. *The Times*, quoted in ibid., p. 31, n. 2.
14. Charles James Fox to Richard Fitzpatrick, 30 July 1798, quoted in John Drinkwater, *Charles James Fox* (London: Ernest Benn, 1928), p. 289.
15. Prince of Wales to the Duke of York, 14 April 1793, in Aspinall (ed.), *Correspondence of Prince of Wales*, vol. 2, p. 348.
16. Prince of Wales to Queen Charlotte, 24 January 1793, in ibid., p. 334.
17. Prince of Wales, in ibid., p. 349.
18. Wraxall, *Memoirs*, vol. 5, p. 36
19. Prince of Wales to Mrs Fitzherbert, quoted in Aspinall (ed.), *Correspondence of Prince of Wales*, vol. 2, p. 443, n. 1.
20. Prince of Wales to Captain J. W. Payne, July 1794, in ibid., p. 442.
21. George III to William Pitt, 24 August 1794, quoted in Earl Stanhope, *Life of the Right Honourable William Pitt,* vol. 2 (London: John Murray, 1861), Appendix, p. xx.

3. LOVING AND HATING

1. Prince of Wales to the Duke of York, 24 July 1791, in Aspinall (ed.), *Correspondence of Prince of Wales*, vol. 2, pp. 174–5.
2. Prince of Wales to the Duke of York, 29 August 1794, in ibid., p. 433.
3. Queen Charlotte to Duke Charles of Mecklenburg-Strelitz, August 1794, in ibid., vol. 3, p. 9.
4. Malmesbury (ed.), *Diaries and Correspondence of James Harris*, vol. 3, pp. 165, 168.
5. Ibid., p. 168.

6. Ibid., p. 196.
7. Ibid., p. 208.
8. Ibid., p. 218.
9. James Harris, quoted in David, *Prince of Pleasure*, p. 169.
10. Queen Victoria's journal, entries for 2 September and 13 November 1838, quoted in Hibbert, *Prince of Wales*, p. 160.
11. Prince of Wales to William Pitt, in Aspinall (ed.), *Correspondence of Prince of Wales*, vol. 3, p. 315.
12. Prince of Wales to William Pitt, in ibid., p. 315.
13. William Pitt, in ibid., p. 320.
14. Prince of Wales to Queen Charlotte, 7 January 1796, in ibid., p. 126.
15. George III to the Prince of Wales, 7 January 1796, in A. Aspinall (ed.), *The Later Correspondence of George III*, vol. 2 (Cambridge: Cambridge University Press, 1963), p. 451.
16. Prince of Wales to the Princess of Wales, quoted in Doris Leslie, *The Great Corinthian: A Portrait of the Prince Regent* (London: Eyre & Spottiswoode, 1952), pp. 125–6.
17. George III to Prince of Wales, 31 May 1796, in Aspinall (ed.), *Correspondence of the Prince of Wales*, vol. 3, p. 194.
18. Prince of Wales's will, written on 10 January 1796, in Aspinall (ed.), *Correspondence of Prince of Wales*, vol. 3, p. 135.
19. Prince of Wales to Lady Rutland, quoted in Hibbert, *Prince of Wales*, p. 171.
20. Prince of Wales, recorded by Baron Glenbervie; quoted in ibid., p. 299.
21. *The Times*, 18 June 1800.
22. Prince of Wales to Lord Moira, quoted in Hibbert, *Prince of Wales*, p. 229.
23. Affidavit by the Prince of Wales, quoted in Hibbert, *Prince of Wales*, p. 240.
24. Princess Elizabeth to the Prince of Wales, 2 August 1797, and Lord Minto to Lady Minto, 1798, in Aspinall (ed.), *Correspondence of Prince of Wales*, vol. 3, pp. 357, 385.
25. Princess of Wales to Lady Townshend, quoted in Joanna Richardson, *The Disastrous Marriage: A Study of George IV and Caroline of Brunswick* (London: Jonathan Cape, 1960), p. 66.
26. Lady Bessborough to Granville Leveson Gower, in Castalia, Countess Granville (ed.), *Lord Granville Leveson Gower (First Earl Granville): Private Correspondence, 1781 to 1821*, vol. 2 (London: John Murray, 1916), pp. 203–4.
27. Quoted in Hibbert, *Prince of Wales*, vol. 1, p. 219.
28. Prince of Wales to Spencer Perceval, 4 February 1811, quoted in Hibbert, *Prince of Wales*, p. 279.

4. REGENT OF STYLE

1. James Greig (ed.), *The Farington Diary*, vol. 7 (London: Hutchinson, 1927), p. 22.
2. 'Drawn Plan of the Tables in the Temporary Room, Carlton House, for the Grand Fête in 1811', in Frederick Crace, *A Catalogue of Maps, Plans, and Views of London, Westminster and Southwark, Collected and Arranged by Frederick Crace* (London: 1878), p. 83.
3. Gioachino Rossini, quoted in Christopher Hibbert, *George IV: Regent and King, 1811–1830* (London: Allen Lane, 1973), p. 266.
4. *The Literary Gazette; and Journal of Belles Lettres, Arts, Sciences, etc.*, 19 February 1821, p. 316.

5. Prince of Wales to Duke of Wellington, quoted in Hibbert, *Regent and King*, p. 293.
6. Ibid., p. 26.
7. Ibid., p. 233.
8. James Stanier Clarke to Jane Austen, quoted in Kristin Flieger Samuelian, *Royal Romances: Sex, Scandal and Monarchy in Print, 1780–1821* (New York: Palgrave Macmillan, 2010), p. 1.
9. Charles Saumarez Smith, *The National Gallery: A Short History* (London: Frances Lincoln, 2009), pp. 19–28.
10. Reeve (ed.), *Greville Memoirs*, vol. 1, p. 240.
11. Ibid., p. 247.
12. George Thomas [Keppel], Earl of Albemarle, *Fifty Years of My Life* (London: Macmillan, 1877), p. 18.
13. Francis Bamford and the Duke of Wellington (eds), *The Journal of Mrs Arbuthnot, 1820–1832*, vol. 2 (London: Macmillan, 1950), p. 369.
14. W. H. Pyne, *The History of the Royal Residences of Windsor Castle, St James's Palace, Carlton House, Kensington Palace, Hampton Court, Buckingham House, and Frogmore*, vol. 3 (London: A. Dry, 1819), 'The History of Carlton-House', pp. 90–92.
15. Alexandra Loske, 'The Decorative Scheme of the Royal Pavilion, Brighton: George IV's Design Ideas in the Context of European Colour Theory, 1765–1845', unpublished PhD thesis, University of Sussex, 2014, p. 172.
16. Ibid., p. 171.
17. Louis J. Jennings (ed.), *The Correspondence and Diaries of the Late Right Honourable John Wilson Croker ... Secretary to the Admiralty from 1809 to 1830*, vol. 1 (London: John Murray, 1884), p. 125; Dorothea Lieven, quoted in Hibbert, *Regent and King*, p. 126; Reeve (ed.), *Greville Memoirs*, vol. 1, p. 54.
18. Reeve (ed.), *Greville Memoirs*, vol. 1, p. 49.
19. Duke of Wellington and Henry Brougham, quoted in Hibbert, *Regent and King*, p. 102.
20. Lady Brownlow, quoted in Percy Fitzgerald, *The Life of George the Fourth*, vol. 2 (London: Tinsley Brothers, 1881), pp. 155–6.
21. James Chandler, *England in 1819: The Politics of Literary Culture and the Case of Romantic Historicism* (Chicago and London: University of Chicago Press, 1998), p. 21, n. 43.

5. KING AT LAST

1. George Canning, quoted in Kevin Gilmartin, *Writing against Revolution: Literary Conservatism in Britain, 1790–1832* (Cambridge: Cambridge University Press, 2009), p. 146.
2. Reeve (ed.), *Greville Memoirs*, vol. 1, p. 12.
3. Ibid., p. 23.
4. Ibid., p. 31.
5. Hibbert, *Regent and King*, p. 153.
6. Ibid., p. 187.
7. Anthony Powell (ed.), *Barnard Letters, 1778–1824* (London: Duckworth, 1928), p. 291.
8. Duke of Wellington, quoted in Hibbert, *Regent and King*, p. 229.

9. Ibid.
10. John Prebble, *The King's Jaunt: George IV in Scotland, August 1822: 'One and Twenty Daft Days'* (London: Collins, 1988), p. 364.
11. Reeve (ed.), *Greville Memoirs*, vol. 1, p. 99.
12. Duke of Wellington, quoted in Hibbert, *Regent and King*, pp. 308–9.
13. Duke of Wellington, *Despatches, Correspondence, and Memoranda*, vol. 5, 1873, p. 518.
14. George IV, quoted in Lionel G. Robinson (ed.), *Letters of Dorothea Lieven during her Residence in London, 1812–1834* (London: Longmans, Green, and Co., 1902), p. 187.
15. Reeve (ed.), *Greville Memoirs*, vol. 1, p. 189.
16. Ibid., p. 209.
17. Hibbert, *Regent and King*, p. 335.
18. Ibid., p. 338.
19. Reeve (ed.), *Greville Memoirs*, vol. 2, p. 1.

Further Reading

It seems at first sight surprising that there are so few biographies of George IV, and that the definitive account remains that of Christopher Hibbert, published in full in two volumes in 1972 and 1973. But there are perhaps two good reasons for this. In the first place, George IV was a monarch whose reputation was low during his reign and never really improved. In the second, the destruction of his collections of bits and pieces and, surely, of much of his private correspondence, both incoming and outgoing, meant that his inner world of emotion and belief is surprisingly hard to reproduce. My own attempts to track down material in some remote or undiscovered corner of the Royal Archive were fruitless. The cull started with the Duke of Wellington soon after George's death. It was probably continued by exasperated royal servants, particularly those of Queen Victoria, who had little time for her uncle. George's letters and his tat, his wardrobe and his jottings seem all to have been burned or binned, leaving only letters to his family, official correspondence and some correspondence that came back to him, from Maria Fitzherbert, for instance. Archives like that of Charles James Fox, which might have contained a good deal of material both by and about him, were also destroyed. Those who seek to preserve reputations generally obliterate the objects of their veneration. Without the personal, the person disappears.

Contemporary accounts of the period remain some of the most vivid. Nathaniel Wraxall's rambling and often mendacious memoirs, in many editions, are gripping. Greville's *Memoirs* offer good close-up observations of politicians and public figures. The Byron industry is still unstoppable, with interest now centred on the women of the Byron and Shelley circles, and on the mathematical and scientific world of Babbage and Ada Lovelace, most recently in Miranda Seymour's *In Byron's Wake* (2018). Leslie Marchand's three-volume *Byron: A Biography* (1957), though fatally dated in the pass it gives the poet's attitudes to women, is still a great read, as are Byron's own letters.

Other members of the royal family, besides George, have belatedly come to the attention of biographers. Flora Fraser's *The Unruly Queen: The Life of Queen Caroline* (1996) was the first modern work to tell Caroline's side of the sorry marital story of the mismatched couple. Janice Hadlow's *The Strangest Family* (2014) lays bare the sad lives of George IV's siblings. Flora Fraser's *Princesses* (2004) concentrated on George's sisters, while my own *A Royal Affair* (2006) put the lives of George III and his siblings in the contexts of the European Enlightenment and the American Revolution.

After years of neglect, the period between the French Revolution and the Victorian age in Britain is now getting the attention it deserves. Alongside existing histories of London by Gerry White and Roy Porter, to name two of the best, we now have more detailed analysis of the mores and life of the city in this period, in particular Vic Gatrell's *City of Laughter* (2006), Ben Wilson's *Decency and Disorder* (2007) and Dan Cruikshank's *The Secret History of Georgian London* (2009). The wider social and economic changes of the period are explored in Richard Holmes's *The Age of Wonder* (2008) and Jenny Uglow's *In These Times* (2015). Putting Britain in a global context and decentring national history is valuable and necessary; Eric Hobsbawm's *The Age of Revolution* (1962) started this process, while Christopher Bayly's *The Birth of the Modern World, 1780–1914* (2004) offers a revisionist account from a different political perspective.

Perhaps the most exciting developments in historiography to enter the realm of public history are coming in the fields of imperial and environmental history, where the costs, both psychic and economic, of empire and industrialization are finally being totted up. The brilliant work of the Centre for the Study of the Legacies of British

Slave-Ownership at University College London, led by Catherine Hall, has lifted the veil from the extent of wealth extraction from the British Empire, and the uses to which it was put. New work on the British in India is finally ripping away the cosy view of empire which for far too long has dominated narrative writing on the subject. Environmental history, which is putting the natural world and the whole earth back into the history of humankind, will have much to say on the period covered by this short book, when a new era in human history, the Anthropocene, was unwittingly inaugurated, and a series of changes begun beside which the lives of monarchs are just the dances of fleas.

Picture Credits

1. Benjamin West, *Queen Charlotte with her Children*, detail, 1779 (Royal Collection Trust © Her Majesty Queen Elizabeth II, 2019/Bridgeman Images)
2. George Stubbs, *George, Prince of Wales*, 1791 (Royal Collection Trust © Her Majesty Queen Elizabeth II, 2019/Bridgeman Images)
3. Richard Cosway, *George, Prince of Wales*, c.1793 (Royal Collection Trust © Her Majesty Queen Elizabeth II, 2019/Bridgeman Images)
4. Richard Cosway, *Maria Fitzherbert*, c.1789 (Royal Collection Trust © Her Majesty Queen Elizabeth II, 2019/Bridgeman Images)
5. Thomas Rowlandson and Augustus Charles Pugin, *Carlton House*, 1809 (Chronicle/Alamy)
6. Thomas Rowlandson, *Presenting the Trophies*, 1815 (Florilegius/Alamy)
7. Richard Carlile (publisher), *The Peterloo Massacre*, 1819 (Classic Image/Alamy)
8. George Cruikshank, *The Cato Street Conspirators*, 1820 (Pictorial Press/Alamy)
9. Charles Williams, *How Happy I Could Be With Either!!*, 1820 (© Trustees of the British Museum)
10. Circle of Thomas Lawrence, *George IV*, 1822 (Private Collection, © Philip Mould Ltd, London/Bridgeman Images)
11. George Hayter, *The Trial of Queen Caroline*, detail, 1820 (National Portrait Gallery, London, © NPG)
12. Richard Cosway, *The Eye of the Prince of Wales*, early 1790s (Private Collection, © Oxford Film and Television Ltd)
13. Rembrandt Harmensz. van Rijn, *Self-portrait*, 1642 (Royal Collection Trust © Her Majesty Queen Elizabeth II, 2019/Bridgeman Images)
14. Aelbert Cuyp, *Evening Landscape with Figures and Sheep*, 1655–9 (Royal Collection Trust © Her Majesty Queen Elizabeth II, 2019/Bridgeman Images)
15. John Nash, *A View of the Royal Pavilion at Brighton*, 1826, published 1827 (British Library, London. © British Library Board. All Rights Reserved/Bridgeman Images)
16. John Nash, *The Chinese Gallery in the Royal Pavilion at Brighton*, 1826 (Cooper Hewitt, Smithsonian Design Museum/Alamy)
17. David Wilkie, *George IV in Highland Dress*, 1830 (Royal Collection Trust © Her Majesty Queen Elizabeth II, 2019/Bridgeman Images)

Acknowledgements

I would like to thank Stuart Proffitt for commissioning this book and editing it in his inimitable way and with his now famous blue pen, the sight of which, instead of striking the usual trepidation, was a tonic. I like to think of myself as well disposed towards modern electronic editing and its concomitant saving of trees and printing ink; but for a dyslexic writer the visual is still easiest. I went through the copy-edited manuscript with paper and screen side-by-side.

I would also like to thank the staff of the Royal Archive and the Royal Collection, in particular Desmond Shawe-Taylor, Surveyor of the Queen's Pictures, who gave me the benefit of his knowledge of George IV's taste in painting and of the Royal Picture collection in its entirety. His understanding of George IV's taste greatly enhanced my own, and I have gratefully used it in describing George's acquisitions when he was Prince of Wales and the improvements and hanging of the collection at Buckingham Palace and Windsor Castle when he was king.

I would like to thank the staff at Penguin, in particular Ben Sinyor and Anna Hervé, along with Kate Parker and Stephen Ryan, and Cecilia Mackay who undertook the picture research. They have suffered my weak spelling and generally cavalier attitude to grammar with fortitude and good humour. Finally I would like to thank those who have tilled this field before me, especially Jenny Uglow, Janice Hadlow, Flora Fraser and the late Christopher Hibbert.

Index

own establishment 14,
16–17; character 15, 15–16,
19, 24, 61; weight 16, 54, 68,
89, 90; attains majority
16–17; income 16–17, 34, 91;
George III's codes of
behaviour 18–19; rebellion
19; political involvement
19–21; extravagance 22,
62–3; love life 24–7, 28; the
Regency Crisis 34–7; private
life 27–8; health 28–9, 90;
marriage to Maria
Fitzherbert 29–34, 40, 85;
debts 31, 40, 62; finances 31,
33–4; drinking 37, 54;
womanizing 37, 40–1, 45,
53–4; portrayal as *A
Voluptuary under the
Horrors of Digestion* 38;
and the French Revolution
39–40; breaks with Maria
Fitzherbert 41–2; marriage
to Caroline of Brunswick 42,
43–7; relationship with
Caroline 46–7, 52–3, 57–8,
83–94; relationship with
press 4–5, 47–8;
correspondence 50–1;
separation from Caroline
52–3; renews relationship
with Mrs Fitzherbert 53–4;
relationship with Princess
Charlotte 57–8; appointed
Regent 60; as Regent 3–4,

61–81; pension bill 63;
patronage 63–4; interest in
music 64–5; reading 65–6;
clothing 67–8; habit of
accumulation 68–9;
Armoury 69; painting
collection 70–1; death of
Princess Charlotte 75–6; and
the Peterloo Massacre
79–80; accession 83; reign
83–96; and Caroline's trial
84–5; coronation 85; and
death of Caroline 86–7; Irish
tour 87–8; Wilkie portrait
89; expenses 91; and
Catholic Relief Act 92–5, 98;
health declines 95–6; death 3,
96–7; will 85, 97; obituary 3;
funeral 97–8; legacy 98–9
Gillray, James 38
Glasgow 49
Goderich, Frederick John
   Robinson, Viscount 92
Godwin, William 80
Göttingen 89
Greenwich 45
Grenville, William Wyndham,
   Baron 55
Greville, Charles 74, 74–5,
   82–3, 83, 90–1, 95–6, 98
Grey, Charles, Earl 55, 84, 99
Grosvenor, Richard, Earl 10

Halford, Sir Henry 97
Hamilton, Mary 24–5